T0149372

"Look Ma We Made It"

Thelma A. P. Krzyszton

iUniverse, Inc.
Bloomington

"Look Ma We Made It"

iUniverse books may be ordered through booksellers or by contacting:

iUniverse
1663 Liberty Drive
Bloomington, IN 47403
www.iuniverse.com
1-800-Authors (1-800-288-4677)

Because of the dynamic nature of the Internet, any web addresses or links contained in this book may have changed since publication and may no longer be valid. The views expressed in this work are solely those of the author and do not necessarily reflect the views of the publisher, and the publisher hereby disclaims any responsibility for them.

Any people depicted in stock imagery provided by Thinkstock are models, and such images are being used for illustrative purposes only.

Certain stock imagery © Thinkstock.

ISBN: 978-1-4759-2783-2 (sc)
ISBN: 978-1-4759-2784-9 (e)

Printed in the United States of America

iUniverse rev. date: 05/23/2012

This Book is dedicated to my parents
Charles and Mary Sawyer
With much love and admiration

You're Loving Daughter

Thelma

Thanks Mom and Dad,
Your encouragement and confidence
In my imagination, has inspired me to write
And to face the many challenges that lay ahead of me.

And to my daughter Barbara, who gave up precious time
With her family, to help her mom get this book ready for the
printers.
Thank You Bunche's (her favorite saying)

Contents

Introduction

We grew up on a dead end street tucked away in a nice little community, in someplace, USA. Here you can find us tucked into our own little corner of the world it was probably safer that way. Most of our formative years were spent wandering in and out of the forests around our house. Our parents felt it was safer to keep us as close to home as possible. Trouble seemed to follow us no matter what we did. With our over active imaginations we could pretend to be whatever put a smile on our face, and a frown on our parents. What a wonderful life we lived hidden away from the real world.

We lived with my Dad's parents whom we loved very much. Being located on a dead-end street was very good for our creative minds giving us multitudes of things to keep us distracted. Which-knowing us was probably the best possible situation for us to be in. The farther away we were from civilization the better. To know us was to love us – or not!

A lot of meals on our dinner table came from the woods behind our home. The vegetables came from working in the neighbor's garden. Times were hard and you did what was necessary to care for your family. Everything we had was obtained through long hours of backbreaking work. My Mom was the best cook ever. She made everything taste so good that leftovers were never an issue in our house. We may not have had very much, but most importantly we had each other. Our very weird sense of humor helped us ease through lean and tough years. But, we learned that if you at least have the gift to love than you have the richest gift a person could ask for. We had plenty of that to go around.

My father is a mechanic, highly skilled in everything from small engines to massive diesel engines. Dr. Charles, MECH, his plaque would read if he had such a thing. He could fix and repair anything on wheels. It didn't matter what it was or who made it, he could fix it. He was and is a master at his work. Yes, folks, that's my dad. Boy, am I proud of him!

Then, there is Mom. Not only was she a wonderful mother, but my best friend as well. We share a lot of common ground together. Talent oozes out of this woman. When she sees something that sparks an interest, she will study it until it is stored away in her memory and go home to duplicate it. There is nothing she can't do; ceramics, painting, sketches, woodworking, dolls, sewing, crocheting, the list goes on forever.

On with the show as they say. See you on the next page.

Boy Meets Girl

The pretty auburn haired beauty was busy at the switchboard, headphones on, directing calls. She receives a call from a young man needing help in finding a number. They exchange some pleasantries, a few laughs, when she tells him she has to get back to work. Not wanting to let her go, he expresses how beautiful her voice sounds, and would love to meet her sometime. Breaking his heart, she tells him that will not happen, and hangs up.

As fate would have it, he was in the right place at the right time, the five and dime malt shop. Sitting at the counter and licking his wounds, she walks in and sits right down beside him; and starts talking to the waitress behind the counter that we called Red. His eyes light up with recognition when he hears her voice. He turns toward her and asks Red to introduce them. "It is nice to meet the face that belongs to the beautiful voice," he says to her. Bingo, he had her undivided attention. This is how Charles met Mary. They talked while she had lunch, and then he walked her back to work. Charles was smitten, Mary had stolen his heart. Now he has to find a way to win hers.

So, for the next couple of days he met her for lunch, and would turn on the charm to sweep her off her feet. He had even proposed marriage, but she turned him down. Then one day he decides to wait out in front of the phone company for her to give her a ride home;

not realizing that her dad always picked her up from work. And to top that off, he parked in the dads normal spot. Oh boy! When Mary came out of work and saw Charles and her dad waiting to pick her up, shear panic covered her pretty face. What to do? She looks at her dad who is in an obvious distraught state, then at Charles and smiles. She chose to get into the car with the young man. Her dad was livid, and followed close behind them all the way to the house. Before Charles could get out of the car to walk Mary to the door, her dad was standing by his door telling him to leave. Then, he yelled at her to get into the house. Charles told her he would call her later.

Mary told him later that her dad had forbid her to see that hoodlum ever again. They laughed and Charles proposed again. This time she said yes. They knew it was not going to be easy because her parents didn't like him but they were determined. So, they set things in motion by getting a marriage license and blood work done. Then, it was time to tell the parents. This would not be an easy task since the dad had already run him off. Now he had to stand in front of the mama and tell her he wanted to marry her daughter. My Grandma was sitting at the table writing letters when they came in and delivered the news. Grandma was so angry, that she slammed her hand down on the table so hard it made the ink bottle fly into the air, and spill all over her letters. Now, she was really mad, and told them to sit down, and don't you dare move until your dad gets here. Oh boy! Grandma called Grandpa, and he was home in record time sending Charles away for the second time. Then he proceeded to lock Mary in the house with no phone privileges for a week. Before Charles left, he told Mary he would call her later. He did try to call her on several occasions but, they hung up when they heard it was him. One day, when Grandma wasn't watching, Mary called Charles at work. She asked him if he still wanted to get married. Hell yes, he says. She tells him to come and get her. He told his boss he was getting married, and he had to go. Charles and his boss were friends, and they had talked about the situation with Mary. His boss told him to go get his bride, and wished him well.

Minutes later he picked up Mary, and took her home to meet his parents. They fell in love with her right away. My Grandma S. gave my aunt some money to buy Mary a dress to wear. That was the day my Mom and Dad got married at the City Clerk's office, with my Aunt and Uncle as witnesses. The following day her parents were at the house demanding to see proof of her marriage. She showed them the license and they were very angry with her, accused her of all sorts of things before they left. She didn't speak to them for a long time after that. It was very hard on Mom to be distant with her parents, she loved them very much. But, she had fallen in love with Dad and wanted to be with him. She hoped someday they would understand and accept him. Looking back I don't think they ever did.

My Amazing Parents

The snow was falling harder now, and Dad was concerned that help would not be able to get to them in time. The weather reports coming over the radio, told of deep snow and blizzard conditions. People were warned to stay home, and not to go out, unless it was an emergency. Mom let out another scream, the pains were getting closer together and poor Dad was getting pretty scared. The nearest phone was a mile up the road, he didn't know if he should leave her alone. What if something should happen while he was gone? Who would help her? After all, they were in an isolated area in the country, and nobody would hear her calls for help.

They didn't have very much protection from the terrible blizzard, and the snow was mounting fast. Looking out the tiny window in the coop, you could barely see the trees, let alone the road. The wind was ripping through the walls, and it was getting harder to keep them warm. The tension and anxiety from trying to make the right decision, was overwhelming. Dad knew he had to react now, before it was too late.

Dad kissed Mom goodbye, and making sure she would be safe, he set off for the phone. My father was very worried that the snow would keep the doctor from coming to help before the baby came. Town was so far away; would the doctor and ambulance be able to get here in time? Dad ran all the way to the phone and back, in hip deep snow. He lost one shoe going, and one shoe on the way back. No time to stop and look for them now, since he had to get back to Mom. By the time Dad had made his way back to the little coop, the doctor was pulling up in the drive. They rushed inside to help Mom, only to find them-selves standing there with their mouths hanging open.

Can you imagine the shocked look on their faces, when they opened the door to find Mom cuddling a beautiful baby boy! It seems that while Dad was running for help, my older brother decided it was time to make his entry into this world of ours. So Mom, being the strong resourceful person she is, pulled herself together, and taking the ribbons from her braids, scalded them and proceeded to deliver the baby by herself. With a lot of determination, she gave our family a new bundle of joy – Bill would be the first of many boys. When the doctor made sure Mom and baby were doing good, he drove them to the hospital, were they made the local news. After Mom and baby were made comfortable, it was time for Dad to relax. He had to recover from his very nerve racking ordeal; it's not easy for dads to have a baby. They go through an awful lot you know, cold feet and all!!

Mom and baby made it to the front page of the morning newspaper, and this is how my grandparents found out. They were going to have a lot of explaining to do. After all this excitement, they found a place in town, and decided to try doing things a little differently, from now on. Dad found work, and things went pretty smooth for about a year. That's when Mom made another trip to the hospital. This time she was a little closer to the delivery room. Well, she made it to the elevators at least! I guess mom's one of those - guess what? Push, push- type of people. She wastes no time fooling around, and she gets out of all those awful preps.

So now we have Billy and Rusty. Russ was the fattest little thing. Hair so long dad had to stop the nurses from braiding it. We were now a family of four. After waiting a reasonable amount of time, oh say, a year, mom was back in the delivery room. AGAIN! This time she got it right! Me, the cutest little baby in the world! Sweet and cuddly, tiny, loveable, etc. (it's my book so I can brag.)

Because of this wonderful miracle, you get to read all about those loveable and adorable children. Not to mention, all the strange and talented people that pop in and out. Boy, are you are in for a treat.

The Grandparents

Two years later Ben was born, and my Dad's parents invited us to live with them. Things were a bit tough all over, and Grandpa needed help with Grandma, and we needed room to run. It turned out to be the best solution for everyone.

My Grandma

My Grandmother was a very heavy lady, and this made getting around a difficult task for her. I believe Grandma was about four foot eleven, and three hundred pounds. She wore a size five shoe, which is not very much to balance all that weight on. It was no wonder she had issues in getting about. Our being there was a help, and relief to my Grandpa.

I saw my Grandma as a very feisty and yet, sweet person but a little shy. I for one was very happy about the move. My Grandmother and I spent a good deal of time together. She would have tea and biscuits or cookies waiting for me after school. As we enjoyed our tea parties, my Grandma would teach me how to be a lady (not a heathen, like when I played with my brothers). How to hold my cup and saucer, with the pinky finger curved as the English do, she saw it on the Television. Where the napkins went, silverware and glasses; always remember to place a napkin on your lap. When Grandma shared her childhood days with me, I would share mine with her.

Those were special times. I guess she liked my company as much as I do. After all, a good listener is hard to find.

Grandmother was either in her rocking chair or propped up in her bed working on something. She had to be busy all the time, didn't like to be idle. My Grandma would make quilts, aprons and a lot of her own clothes. She always wore one of her aprons over her dresses, her hair pulled back into a bun. I can still picture Grandma with glasses perched on her nose busily working away on one of her projects. I guess you could say, at least I could; Grandma was the best quilt maker this side of heaven. She loved her work as if each piece had a life of its' own. Hours would be spent cutting out tiny little shapes, and then sewing them together by hand. Tiny stitches in straight lines, better than a machine. Her quilts lasted for years, and she was very proud of her work. I loved to help her organize all the pieces into separate piles, making it easier for her to pick the one needed. Sometimes she would let me cut them out. She loved spending the time teaching me how to sew and be creative. I treasure those times with Grandma, they were the best. Grandma always told me that when it was time for her to go to Heaven I was to have her favorite goose feather pillow. She wanted me to have something to remember her by. When I was ten, I came home from school to find *the* pillow on my bed. A chill ran down my spine and tears burst forth like a dam had broken free. I ran downstairs to Grandma's room only to find that she was gone. They took her away from me while I was away at school, I would never see or talk to her again. Mom rushed into the room behind me, wrapping her arms around me she held me tight trying to comfort me. She told me that my Grandma had gone home to be with God where she would never be sick again. My heart felt like it had a big hole in it because, I didn't get to say goodbye. I will always remember her patience and sweet sounding gentle voice telling me how much she loved me. To me she will always be the Rembrandt of the Quilting set, and best Grandma ever. We learned a good deal about life and love with Grandma and Grandpa too.

My Grandpa

Grandpa always tried to enjoy life to its' full measure. Loved most people and dogs and he got along with just about everyone. He had quite a hankering for heavy women too! You could hear him bragging about it all the time. He'd say "There was more to love and squeeze." Must have been true; look at my Grandma.

Grandpa and Dad were blessed with terrible tempers. Life would be going along without a care in the world, then wham, they would be out of control. Mom and Grandma calmed them down as best they could but, it was not an easy task. They never saw eye to eye on very many things; this was probably due to the fact that both suffered from the stubborn and bull headed disease. In their world they were right and the other one was an idiot. Don't get me wrong, they loved each other very much. We all know you can't have two boss' in one house they will butt heads.

When my Grandpa was a young boy, he lost his right leg. He fell while walking around in the dump and his knee landed on a broken bottle. The cut was very deep and got infected. The infection was so bad that the Doctors had to remove his leg. At that time, the only thing available was a solid wood leg. He had to learn how to get around with a stiff leg, which he did quite well. When Grandpa was an adult, he traded it for one with a bendable knee; that he never bent. By the time they came out with the bendable knee, Grandpa was so used to swinging his leg to get it to go, he couldn't get used to the other way.

We all think that this may have had an adverse effect on his driving ability. Grandpa drove a truck, with a stick shift. He made boxes, and flats for the greenhouses, and private customers. This was a side job from the shop where he worked during the day. I went along so I could read the road signs for him. His eyesight was not as good as it used to be.

Now, riding in the truck with Grandpa was not your normal everyday experience. I mean, you really had to be there to appreciate the invention of the automatic car. Unless of course it's normal to ride in the truck with your eyes all bulged out, your knuckles turning white, and thoughts of going to the bathroom running through your mind. Frozen stiff and wondering why you said yes in the first place. Is it the last ride I will ever take? You can't escape by closing your eyes, because you have to read the road signs. You're trapped! He picks up the wooden leg and drops it on the gas pedal. (It couldn't be the left leg, could it?) Then he pushes in the clutch, turns on the key, lifts up on the clutch, not gently. The force of it throws you on the floor, and you sort of wonder why you got up. By the time we're in third gear I am looking for the flight pattern, hoping there aren't any red lights up ahead. Stopping is worse than starting. That man could stop on a dime, honest! I mean, when you drop that wood leg down on something, it's down for the count. He picks it up with his hand, moves it over to the new dropping point, and bombs away! And after you've picked your teeth off the windshield you sort of look over at Grandpa with his smiling face, and force your own face to smile, while you tell him how much fun you're having and hope you can do this again. "I have some more deliveries tomorrow" "Oh; that would be super." (All the while thinking; I was afraid of that)

Grandpa had a delivery to make, and as usual I went along to read the signs. While we were on our way to the customer's house, Grandpa told me about the man's dog. He said that she just had a litter of pups, and was very protective of them. He wanted me to stay close by his side, just in case there was a problem. We were walking up to the house, when she come flying around the side of the house, heading straight at us. I jumped behind Grandpa and held on tight. Grandpa told me to stay put and not to worry.

She caught up to us and tried to take a bite out of his leg. Thank goodness it was the wood one. That had to have been quite a shock for her. She yelped, and ran back where she came from. Grandpa looked at his leg, and saw the teeth marks the dog left. He looks at me and winks, "That's going to be a good story to tell." You know, I heard that dog never bit anyone again, tamest dog you ever saw. Made the owner a little mad, but you can't have everything in life.

Everyone should have a Grandfather like mine was, with his suspenders, crooked walk, and his never met a person he didn't like attitude. He was so full of love, and life. Grandpa enjoyed it when

I would sit on his lap and get his pipe ready for him. First you had to pick it up from the ashtray turn it over and give it a little tap to empty the ashes, then I would open the can of Prince Albert tobacco and fill his pipe. You had to do it just right, put in a little and tap not punch it down, then more till it was full. I would hand it to Grandpa for his inspection and if all was well he would light it up. That would make me smile to know I did it right and made him happy. Once he was puffing away I would lean against him and we would spend time together talking about our day.

Grandpa liked to get my momma going by lecturing her on how I was dressed. He would point out that I was a girl and should wear dresses not pants like the boys. Mom would retaliate with how much of a tom boy I was and dresses would get ruined. After awhile against her better judgment Mom would relent and put me in a dress. After Mom and Grandma had to sew my dresses back together a few times I went back to wearing pants. Grandpa would let it go for awhile then he would give Mom grief again. Grandpa just liked to get her all wound up and sputtering; then he would lean back in his chair with a big smile plastered on his face. Mom and Grandpa were always bantering back and forth. It was all done in fun never in anger. He had a great deal of respect for Mom because it was no easy task keeping my Dad in line.

My Grandpa was a special man that I will always cherish. Between Him and my Grandma I learned a lot about unconditional love. When he went away to join Grandma it was like losing my best friend.

Grown-Ups Like to Play Too

Parents always have two sides. The one you met earlier and the one's your about to meet, so hold on now, you're in for a treat. People may say, "She made it up." But then, they are entitled to their opinion, however wrong it is. Some of us have fun and crazy parents and some of us didn't luck out! What can I say? You'd really have to of been there to fully appreciate our parents, and understand their actions. Being quite frank, I still don't!

My parents learned early in their relationship the best way to cope with life's ups and downs. You can only do what is humanly possible everything else has to go on the back burner for another day. The type of people you surround yourself with hearts of gold, always willing to help anyone and everyone. Because of their over-enlarged hearts they were constantly helping stray kids that had no place to turn. Mom and Dad would help them get on their feet with much needed love and guidance. Most of them found that life indeed could be a beautiful thing after all. We had quite the extended family because of this.

They also like to have fun, and party. Most of their parties started out when people would pop over to say, HI! And then a few more, and before you knew it, it was party time! They had great parties. Most of the people who came over played an instrument. We had a piano that Dad had picked up for my lessons; mom played the guitar, and was pretty good. Patty would play the piano when she was over, and she was fantastic. Never read a note, played by ear. Not actually by her ears. She did use her fingers. And boy! Did they fly over those Ivory's. I was always amazed every time I watched her play. I was learning to play, and she was what I wanted to become. Patty made those notes dance to any tune she wanted. Boogie woogie, Country, Waltz, anything. Anyway, by the time everyone got busy on their own special instrument, you'd be looking for the roof to fly away. (Misfortune always seems to strike. The Piano fell through the floor one day, and we had to sell it. I think someone was trying to tell me something.)

On one occasion when the party had moved to the garage, it had gotten pretty dark out and Dad had forgotten to put the cover over a very deep hole by the corner of the garage. Everybody was having fun and the party was in full swing when one of the guests enquired as to where one could find relief. Dad instructed him to go to the door, turn right, and watch out for the hole. And if he made it that far the rest would be easy.

A few minutes later they heard this horrible scream. Thinking they were hearing things they didn't investigate right away. A few minutes later another scream, this time more urgent. Deciding it wasn't their imagination they went to see what's up, and there he was bobbing up and down in the hole. The hole was about six inches deeper then he was and filled with water. Dad say's to him, "I told you to watch out for the hole." He told dad he thought it was a puddle, and stepped right into it, next thing he knew he was learning how to bob for air and scream.

We liked these parties, with all the happy people, dancing and laughing, and just plain having a ball. We would sit upstairs and look between the beams and watch them. They thought we were asleep. Hah! (Who could sleep?) We would not only sit and watch them at play, but were busy planning our strategy on how to invade there world. It took most of our time figuring out who we sent in first. When all the plans were ready, we checked to see how the grownups were doing before we sent in our secret agent.

This time I had to go first, I had the short straw. I was so nervous because I had to keep a close watch on the grownups. My eyes are everywhere, looking, searching out my goal. Counting them to make sure my mission would be possible. Plenty, good, I grab one, nobody would suspect one missing. Move back through the crowd trying not to attract attention to myself. Ease myself to the stairs, climbing slowly, sleepily so no one suspects anything. At the top of the stairs I can breathe again, success. I find my way into the bedroom where they are all waiting my return. I pull it out and Bill opens it, then we pass it around. The four of us sitting there drinking stolen beer. For shame! Everyone wants to know why they don't hear anything from us? "They sure are being good about going to bed, lots of trips for water, and the bathroom."

My mission completed it was Russell's turn to go into the grownups camp, and bring back another beer. Fortunately for us it didn't take much and we were asleep for the night. Thank goodness we didn't do this very often. This could be why we had very little interest in it later in life.

Mom gets busy

Now that you've met part of my family and their friends, let me enlighten you a little, it gets worse. These things of amusement happened beyond our formative years of life. Of course you have to understand that it was all hearsay, that we became formative that is. Some think it was a fluke of fate. I feel it was inevitable that one day we would turn the corner and run headlong into stability. Others are still shaking their heads with wonder and doubt. The rest we haven't been able to convince yet, but we haven't given up, where there's hope, we follow.

I think it would be appropriate if we started with one of Mothers goofs first. Gasp!! Yes Virginia, mom's make boo boos too! Try as they may, to hold a spotless record it does happen to the best of them. Mine was one of the best, and she's still undergoing treatment for fits of hysteria and mass delusion brought on by her precious children.

This first episode concerns Dad teaching her to ride his motorcycle, or bike as we all fondly called those hot muffled, noisy, heavy and a blast machines.

Before humiliating Mom, you should know about the shape of our driveway. It makes the humiliation worth it. This is very important to the teaching program. I'd guess it to be about three hundred feet in length and about seventy-five feet in width. It is a straight driveway that ends at the road just like any other normal drive. On the other side of the drive across the street is a very large ditch, beyond that a once very nicely kept lawn. A small parking lot would have fit nicely in our driveway.

On with the story, I'll try to be gentle Mom. You would think that a driveway of this magnitude would be able to accommodate a small bike now wouldn't you? Wrong!

We aren't sure when it started to go bad for Mom. Dad insists it was the moment she sat on the seat and asked where the gear shift was, and then proceeded to yell contact! Or maybe the wind blowing in her hair, and the sound of the motor revving up got to her. We never found out what went wrong, all we knew was that something sure enough had.

She rode off down the driveway weaving only a minimum amount. When she got to the end of the drive she forgot how to turn it. All the instructions flew right out of her head. So, instead she yells "Whoa, Whoa I say". My Dad is running after her trying to explain in the simplest terms that, "It's not a horse use the brake." - Too late.

Across the street she went, down through the ditch and up into the yard, where the bike laid down and died - Mercifully. This is when Mom stands up and with her dazzling smile, says, "Let's do it again, I think I'm getting the hang of it."

After this it took great courage on Dad's part to look into her sweet little face and say, yes, you can try again." Dad wasn't at all sure he was doing the right thing in teaching her to ride, but he was brave. Just like a real trooper he was.

She was finally ready for the big day, the highway, main roads with cars and people. Dad felt she wouldn't be any readier. He'd been working round the clock and sure she could handle anything out there. On the highway you don't encounter nice, sane people. For some reason when you slip behind a steering wheel, you have a Jekyll and Hyde personality take over. This was what she was up against.

Dad was pale, but we were starting to get used to his new look. He was her passenger as she drove. At her first traffic light Mom came to a stop like a pro. My dad put his feet down to rest while waiting for the light to turn. (Dad has very long legs; they need a lot of rest) The light turned green, but Dad wasn't prepared for what happened next. Mom left him standing in the intersection with the rest of the traffic, and a few hysterical drivers pointing at dad and laughing. It was the first time in quite some time that Dad had color return to his face. It was very becoming. Mom improved with age, and loads of practice. The key word to her success was patience, hers, not Dads.

Next to my uncle; who shall remain nameless so I will just call him Uncle. It keeps the court docket clear. Mom was first-class, but then next to Uncle anyone could have done a better job.

Anyway Uncle was one of Dad's unsuccessful stories. He really doesn't like to be reminded of this failure to communicate sign language. In time were hoping he'll be able to cope with his failure. So we humor him by not mentioning you know who in front of him. Especially, since he doesn't have a long line of successful students. (Remember Mom) But look what he had to work with. It's quite understandable Dad, you can take Mom out of the corner now.

Our Uncle climbed aboard the bike; so far so good. Then he put his hands on the handle bars, this also was good. But when at last he started the bike, which took a little encouragement on his part, he started to have just a little bit of trouble. Not too much, just a bit. He took off down the drive veered off in the wrong direction, and ended up in my neighbor's yard. This in itself isn't the bad part; this was pretty good considering that he was still on the bike and not straddling it like one of my Dad's other students. So he was doing well up until this point. Then he made a little mistake, he sort of bumped into our neighbor's picnic table. It was a sight to see. The bike went one way and he went the other, when finally, we still don't know how to this day, the bike found its way back to the road.

I guess Uncle needless to say flunked riding school, but being the trooper he was, kept on trying until the bike convinced him otherwise. He now rides on very rare occasions. Fortunately, and speaking for all the pedestrians in the world, we thank you.

Harley's

My Dad, I believe had his greatest time riding his bike or working on them. Don't worry; he didn't belong to any gang. He worked on it, rode it, and took pride in it. He gave us rides all the time. This we enjoyed very much. We couldn't wait to get up there behind him and enjoy the wind hitting us in the face.

Dad being a mechanic did servicing on his friends bikes also. He let a couple of the guys use his garage, so they could work on their bikes. To make some side money, he would take on outside work too; with us, he needed help with the doctor bills.

I can still picture him in the summer walking around with his work cap on, his motorcycle boots, and Bermudas. He had very skinny legs and the results were kind of funny. We didn't dare laugh in front of him, because of the amount of time it took Mom to get Dad into Bermudas in the first place. Dad was quite the Don Wan in his day, ladies man and all. Of course that ended when Mom entered the picture and tamed him. I know it's hard to envision this after the skinny legs description but, tis true non-the less.

Dad was on his Harley riding it up and down the driveway, and having a great time doing it. He just kept going back and forth, up and down the drive. We thought for awhile there we had pushed him over the brink. Until on one trip up the drive he accidently bumped into the corner of the garage. (That's what Dad said, you know how the old boo boo stories go) He bit the dust when the little bitty Harley stopped, and he didn't. After his encounter with the garage he didn't get on the Harley for awhile. You have to get your confidence back after a thing like that.

Payday or Not

My Dad had a way with bill collectors. They knew we never had any money, but they insisted on asking for hand outs anyway. They would stop by, or call and Dad would see if they were going to be nasty or nice, kind of like Santa. If nasty, then he'd tell them that he wouldn't put their bill in the hat that week. That's my Dad. Actually our filling cabinet for bills was the pot belly stove in the dining room. If you can't pay, there's no sense looking at them and getting depressed, plus they made good fuel for the stove. If they were serious about getting their money, they always sent another bill. Good old file thirteen, that's what Dad called it. The collectors usually treated him nice after they found out about the hat and they would give him time to pay. I don't know if they thought the bunch of us were in need of strait jackets, or if hearing "Charlie's morgue; you stab'um we slab'um" on the other end of the line and the hat bit gave them a kind streak. Whatever, it usually worked.

The Great Water Fight

It was a hot humid summer day, and Mom and Dad's friends were over. We were all sitting around the kitchen table trying not to be bored out of our minds. Suddenly, out of nowhere one of them threw an ice cold glass of water on someone's back. Then somebody else threw one, it didn't take long before everyone was in the act. We were watching them jump around, screaming, while another was attacked with water. It was on now, pitchers and buckets of water flying all over the kitchen. Someone found our squirt guns and used them on us. Another missed their target and the water went flying out the window landing on an innocent passerby, we think it was Billy. The next thing we knew the garden hose was coming through the window spraying everyone that moved. Picture this all happening in the kitchen. When we were all exhausted from laughing and cool enough, we cleaned up the mess, and what a mess it was. Not being able to top that, they settled down at last.

Looking at all the drowned grownups after their play time was great. We decided to take into consideration that they were under a great deal of pressure. They were not responsible for their actions at this time. It would go down in the books of history as a moment of insanity. But, we all know the truth, now, don't we?

After play time we all know what comes next- *CLEAN UP TIME*. This took a lot of mopping, bailing and a lot of grumbling. But, success was not that far away, and before we knew it, dry land appeared. (They thought our games were silly and stupid, but they forgot they invented them; we were just carrying on with tradition.)

After the kitchen was put in order again, Mom made a batch of her fantastic fudge. She could whip together the most mouth watering fudge you've ever tasted. Melts in your mouth, and drives your taste buds absolutely crazy! We never could copy her recipe, tried for years, and it still doesn't turn out like moms. You either had to eat it with a spoon or use a pick axe on it. If we got hungry for it, we just went home and sweet talked Mom into making some for us. Sure do miss that fudge.

Stupid Radio

As I said earlier, my folks are fun loving, and there are times when they actually act a good deal like us, as you have probably noticed already. My mom and cousin Jim got into it over the stupid radio. Well, I can't say for sure if the radio is stupid or not. I mean it can't exactly tell me now can it? Well, anyway, Jim kept turning the station. Mom would put it on one station, and he'd get right up and turn it to a different one. She preferred country music, and he was for rock n' roll. This went on for a couple of minutes until moms temper was at the boiling point. She picked up the first thing closest to her and threw it at him. Unfortunately for Jim, it was the cat- poor cat. Of course Jimmy didn't feel too good either, but he did ask for it. I mean, he didn't ask for the cat, but he did ask for trouble. He just got what he asked for, didn't he!?

Our Imaginary Friends

Mom, her friend Sandy, and I would sit in the dining room most of the time and talk. Their hubby's were always busy taking cars apart or motorcycles, whatever the case may be. And then of course, you had to put them back together again. It helps them run better that way. It was pretty dull full time work. They were like master surgeons at work. Only, they didn't get sterilized every time they had to do surgery. Can you picture it; sterilized garages, popping up all across the Country. It wouldn't catch on very fast, those sterilized tools could be a little too hot to handle.

Now back to what I was leading up to. The ladies would get so bored, and I'd watch them getting bored. (I was in training for when I got married.) To pull them out of their rut, I invented an imaginary friend and game. I called my friend, Igor. My favorite character in all those monster movies I watched all the time.

Igor caught on real fast, and before long Mom and Sandy had little friends also. Mom's friend was Fred, and Sandy's was Herman. We developed them into their own personalities, and gave them chores to do. We would sit around the table talking with them. It got a little weird, but always very interesting.

The men folk not knowing of our latest additions to the family; walked right into a car race on the dining room ceiling, with our friends as the drivers. Our heads were all going around in circles, and we were cheering them on, and shouting encouragements at them. The guys were ready to call the Looney bin for us. But, they were afraid nobody would believe them. Would you?

My Dad, the courageous one, leaned over the table and looked directly up, he was curious. He shook his head and looked at each of us slowly, turned to the guys and shook his head again. When he looked back at us we said, "Herman won!"

That did it, back to the garage. We were still bored after this because the guys were afraid it was catchy. So we carried our little friends around with us and tried to at least have some fun. Mom would head out the door and give a call for Fred. "Fred, don't sit in the sugar bowl, you know we don't like eating fur balls" and "Igor, stop fighting with Herman, you know he can't defend himself, and besides your bigger than he is," "He is not!" "Fred put that back", and on it went, for days and then weeks. Then, one day, they just seemed to disappear as quickly as they had appeared. Poof!!

Roll Playing

I think somewhere along the line roles were changed on occasion. For some reason we would walk into a room to find the grownups throwing pillows; toys, odd sorts of paraphernalia (good word huh) at each other. When they would notice they had a full audience, they would go into their routine of pretending to be cleaning or rearranging the furniture, anything they thought our young minds would buy. Very interesting how when you throw stuffed pillows just right you could knock down half a dozen cobwebs, and dust a lamp as it swishes past on the way to the floor. Never worked for us, must be just for the grownups.

They would try to use psychology on us, but it never worked. We had them figured out before we were three, but they insisted on trying to outsmart us. A child's mind holds a world of things locked away in their own little compartments, just waiting for the right time to come out, and trip up a grownup. You must remember to think like a child if you want to be in the game.

The Babies Just Keep Coming

Two years later mom did it again! Yes you guessed it, another baby. Why, we don't have a clue. You would have thought their nerves couldn't handle anymore of us. This ride to the Hospital was fun too! My Uncle Cecil had to drive mom to the hospital. Only one problem, he was a very bad driver, only drove when necessary. This unfortunately fell under that term, necessary. They had quite a struggle getting out of the driveway, let alone to the hospital. They finally had a break when he eventually got underway, the tire went flat. I believe this to be a blessing in disguise. This allowed them to seek desperately needed help somewhere else. So Mom and Uncle Cecil hitched a ride from the neighbor to where my Dad worked. He was only eight blocks from our house. Dad borrowed the company truck and took Mom to the hospital. It's not every day that an expectant mother shows up at the hospital in a tow truck!

She has a flare for it don't you think. I guess it takes a knack for doing it the right way. No humdrum baby births in our house. No Siree! Do it right, or don't do it at all, I always say. The more screwed up the better.

This was another boy, and they named him Vincent Peter. Five now, poor Mom, how will she ever survive, how will she keep up? She must be feeling like a baby machine by now. I can just picture her looking up and saying, "Why me? I've been good. Are there anymore? OH NO!!!"

Mom let us help spoil him, and take care of him. We took turns holding and fighting over who did last. I learned how to fold diapers, it was easy. Mom deserved our help; she needed the rest from us. In fact, we needed a rest from us. It's hard work keeping up your image. But, unfortunately, it didn't take long for the newness of helping with the baby to wear off, and we were at it again. What did you expect? Miracles!

We went back to running through the laundry with muddy hands, and tracking up the just washed floors. Bumping into fly paper and getting our hair caught. You look pretty silly standing there with this long sticky thing covered with flies stuck to your head, screaming, HELP!!!! Then you spend weeks washing your hair to get the sticky stuff out. It was an experience you wouldn't want to try more than once. After this you spend the rest of your life walking with your knees bent so that fly papers can't grab you. Could be that fly papers could be used for more than flies, huh? Mom's can be pretty creative .

Again, really?

Well, Mom's been busy again, she said this one was an oops! Right! We knew better. We've heard all those stories about where the baby comes from. You can't fool us. Birds and bees, the rabbits, and of course, no story is not complete unless you hear about the cabbage patch. But, they like to keep us young and innocent. So, we play along with them so that we don't spoil their fun.

This oops turned out to be another boy. Actually, someone has a market on baby girls, because their always out when it's our turn. I would have thought that after six memorable trips to the hospital that they could scrounge up a little bitty girl for us to take home. But - *no* we get yet another boy, so in giving it considerable thought, I have come to the conclusion that it really doesn't matter what I want. Mom and Dad picked him out I will just have to deal with it. Brother number five was given the name of Thomas Mitchell, now that does have a nice sound to it, maybe I could learn to love him even if he is a boy.

Tom was not like the rest of us. I think he was imported. He was QUIET. He kept to himself, behaved (most of the time at least) you'd have to send out search party's to find him. Smoke signals came in handy at times. Unless it was dinner time, then he was half an hour early. That boy had a nose like a bloodhound; he could smell food a mile away, even if it was canned.

A little insight into my Dad, who after going through quite a few births with mom, started taking vacations when she went to the hospital. When Tommy was born, Dad went hunting and mom went to the hospital. (Of course labor started after he was gone, but that's no excuse) This wasn't an agreed upon thing, it just turned out that way. When we contacted him about the coming event, he said he had every confidence that Mom knew exactly what to do, he'd be home when she was, and have nice time. When Jimmy was born, Billy went to the hospital with Mom. We went to a drive-in with pop (dad). Billy needed the experience anyway. He was grand. At least that's what I heard. He paced the floor and smoked like a fiend grabbing every nurse in sight for information. We were so proud of him, a real trooper, just like Dad would have been.

After seven children, there just isn't anything knew for the father to be to do. They need to create a different type of waiting room for expectant fathers. Like, putting a pool table in one corner, a pinball machine in another, and say, a poker table in another one, and most important, a TV set. And they should definitely put in a cigar machine and vending machines for snacks and drinks.

I guarantee if you do all of the above, you won't be able to get rid of them. You'll have expectant fathers lining up to get in. They'll have to take a number. And they'll have to punch a time clock to make sure that when the new Mom leaves they do too! Ask any new daddy to be and see if I'm right. Of course you're going to get your usual amount of daddy's that are going to fake it. Just to see what it's like and if it would be worth the trouble. So careful screening will be necessary.

Ever meet a father that didn't have to bend over backwards to make the new mama happy? The ones that don't are too busy with their own morning sickness. They didn't have the time to worry about the blimp that can't get out of the chair and or stole their slippers.

They have to supply all the fixings for strange cravings as well. Don't matter to them if you have to bundle up in the middle of the night, and chase all over town to find it. Mom had a craving for hot fudge sundaes. Well, try finding a Dairy Queen open in the middle of January. They know when to close up for the season. Which is more than some can say. Dad was so engrossed in his search for the Dairy Queen (and a few friends who thought it would be fun to hunt for it) that by the time he actually found one, it was in Toledo, Ohio. Really mother! (I think this episode speaks for all of us, don't you?)

Not only do they supply the goodies, but they have to sacrifice their clothes and their prize bedroom slippers. When Moms seventh month arrived Dad would automatically hand over his slippers, dropping a tear out the corner of his eye. Then he would wonder if he would ever get them back before the seams split from the swelling. Oh well, the sacrifices one must make for the sake of comfort!!

A few years later we were blessed with yet another boy. This one was called Jimmy. I remember when they were leaving for the hospital, I told them not to bring home anymore boys. Mom said it wasn't up to her and, we had to take what we get. I told her if it's a boy send it back. Like that would be possible, but then to a fourteen year old it made perfect sense. So, after a few hours had passed Mom called from the hospital to tell me how sorry she was and that I had another brother. Why are they always out when we get there? But, he was cute and cuddly so I guess we can keep him too. I am never going to get a baby sister, to share my room clothes and toys. Wait a minute, what am I thinking, bring on the boys', share my stuff, not on your life.

A few days later, Mom came home from the hospital with Jimmy and apologized again. I told Mom it was ok, by now I have come to terms with the idea that I was to be an only girl. Especially, after the light bulb went off finally. Jimmy became my little tag-a-long. He loved his big sis. When he was two he had times of being the big pain in the neck too. Like when he'd go thru my things and find my camera or something else that he shouldn't have found. I still to this day have two of the most gorgeous pictures of my curtains. Or the time he grabbed my glasses and pulled them apart. How in the world does a two year old have enough oomph to break glasses? Or when he was four and he decided that my Volkswagen needed a good cleaning by sticking a hose in the window and let the water run till my car was flooded. Good thing it was a Volkswagen, no carpet! I opened the door and flooded the driveway. After I wiped it all down it was pretty clean.

But the biggest thing I remember is when just after I was married. I think it was a couple of days after and I'd gone over to see Mom. Jimmy answered the door, and hollered into mom, "It's that lady again. " Let this be a lesson to the elderly, even four year olds can forget who you are.

Billy, Russ and I were in our teens when Jimmy joined our family. Russ was always busy with his friends. I was fourteen and was better known to him as the *babysitter*. A few years went by and Bill enlisted in the Army, so he wasn't around very much, and we missed him a lot. So the younger kids; Vince, Ben and Jimmy had to find ways to keep themselves entertained. They were probably better off not having us in charge. They were a whole lot more tolerable than we could ever be. It was about time Mom caught a break.

Are You Sure Their Mine?

Children develop their own personalities at an early age, we all had ours. Unfortunately, some of us developed better than the others. Just kidding folks! We all needed to try again. They say if you keep on trying you'll eventually get it right. I don't think so. Some things are perfect the first time out. (Like us)

Looking back on all the things we did, I think my mother must have had nerves of steel. How else was she able to handle us? Mom used to tell us all the time, "You just wait till your children get into things, then you'll see what I'm yelling about." We didn't understand this at the time. For one thing we didn't have children, and didn't want any, and for another we were only five, six, and seven. But as the years rolled on, and she would repeat what she said, it started to sink in deeper and deeper, along with fear. Today, I know what she meant, and repeat it often myself.

The Instant Sitter. (Priced to sell low)

All you need is a clothesline pole, clothesline and imagination. Lord knows we have plenty in our house. Hook one end of the line to the pole, the other to one of us, or all three, and presto! Instant Sitter. Give us a few toys, or a tub for our pool, and we were content for hours. Sometimes we even had the sprinkler to run threw or sit on. Believe me, it's ideal. I think she should patent it.

I can hear you now; cruel, inhuman, sell me one, etc. It was merciful! Don't be hard on Mom; it was her only line of defense against us. You should have had the pleasure of seeing us in action, think about it. We had the minds of geniuses. I don't blame her. (It was her or us.) On the contrary, I recommend her for the highest award given in combat. We actually felt sorry for her. (Well, maybe a little bit I don't want to go aboard with the pity, image control.)

I myself would have used her idea except that I didn't have any poles. And when I did, the neighborhood kids tore them down two weeks after I dug five foot holes in clay to put them in. We live in a Quiet neighborhood.

We liked it really, and besides, what is better? Use The Instant Sitter or the need to punish your kids every five minutes? Give or take a couple. I preferred Mom's way. Your probably yelling "Beat them, beat them all! Run while you can, get away, flee.)

Laundry Surprises

My brothers were a unique bunch, and they unfortunately liked to collect all kinds of little things to store in their pockets. My mother would get quite a shocker when it was wash day. I mean, reaching into someone's pocket, and finding a couple of worms, assorted bugs, soft bubble gum, one time a live frog! And of course the time she put the pants thru the wringer and flattened out a garter snake. It made a nice belt if you like those kinds of things.

After the initial shock, and a queasy stomach, mom would venture on with the laundry. I'd catch her picking up the pocket by the very tip, and dumping it, to see if it was safe to touch. It's risky business to do children's laundry, especially boys stuff.

We kept her on her toes all the time, never stopping to rest, or to catch a glimpse of sanity. "Are all the kids this way?" She would ask. "It must have been a full moon, or maybe a spell. Could be a dream! Let it be a dream, please." No such luck. I doubt that I would have volunteered for her job.

Boys and Toys

We were busy little bees getting into things. Very curious, wanting to know what made things go, and so on; like the boys toys. They would get a toy and immediately hide in their dissecting room (their closet) so they could dissect it. Had to know what made it tick.

They dissected my doll. I received it for Christmas one year. Mom and Dad had saved for a long time to buy it for me, and it was a beauty. Three feet tall with an evening gown, hi-heels, jewelry-amazing! I really loved that doll. It was the prettiest thing anyone had ever given me. Then, it came up missing. I told Mom and Dad that someone had kidnapped my doll. A search party was formed immediately. We searched the house from top to bottom. Any guesses where we found it? That's right! It was in their dissecting room. Way in the back of the closet under some junk, it was mutilated beyond repair. I won't go into detail what they did to it, except to say that they were extremely messy.

I'd had the doll for such a short time. The only pleasure I received from it, was to see the boy's get what they had coming to them. They didn't find sitting very comfortable for awhile. They said they felt terrible about what they had done, and it was not because they got caught and punished. That didn't have a thing to do with it. I was their baby sister. Since they are my brothers, I forgave them.

Snow in the Kitchen

My Mom loved to bake. She was always in the kitchen making bread or cakes something wonderful. Mom kept her flour in a large can in the kitchen. She felt it was easier to store and keep this way. Under normal conditions, she would have been right. She kept a lot on hand, because of all the goodies. I'd say around fifty pounds or so.

So one day while Mom was outside hanging up clothes to dry, we were in a mischievous mood, again. One of our worst I should think. We opened the can, looked inside, and out it swooshed, covering us from head to toe. Honest, we only looked. Well, ok, maybe we touched it a little bit, but just a little. We looked like someone had mistaken us for chicken, and dipped us for the fryer.

By the time Mom came back in for another load of laundry, the kitchen looked like winter wonderland. We knew we were in for it. You can usually tell by the color red Mom turned, as to what shade your bottom was going to end up. Mom came in, looked, and couldn't speak. That was a bad sign already. She left the room and came back with the camera, took our picture (evidence in case the punishment went haywire we figured) then let us have it. You ever notice that they have to have the pictures. Why is that? Proof in case you go to court and need to plead insanity. The judge would let her go and book us.

Also, this way you can show your friends how dumb your children are. And you can look sweet and give a little smile and say to them, "These are my little darlings having a little midwinter bake, aren't they sweet?" So smile while you're able, then run and hide before she sets the camera down.

The breakfast table was a very adventuresome place in our house. A place filled with the noise, and laughter of a new day. It was very much like Grand Central Station. In fact, that's what Mom nick named our happy home.

Everyone was always dashing around in a hurry to go nowhere. And of course there were the usual discussions about school, chores, who feeds the animals today, and what to do with the food. In most homes you eat it, if it is a normal home. But we aren't dealing with your average run of the mill family. More like Looney tunes!

Bill and Russell usually fed the dogs under the table. Benny preferred to load up his spoon with oatmeal, or cornmeal, and zap everyone. His zapping was getting to us, every few minutes you could hear someone yell "Duck!"

At one of these joyous occasions, he had a surprise. We were having our hot cocoa, toast and oatmeal when Benny got bored and started zapping. I'm guessing that Grandfather had enough, so he took his bowl of cereal, Bens, and he turned it upside down on Benny's head. Grandpa turned the bowl a few times so it would get stuck in his hair. He did it with such grace and swiftness; we were all very much impressed. We didn't think Grandpa had it in him.

The startled look on Ben's face should have been captured on film. Where was the camera now MOM! Poor Benny, he never zapped again. His zapper had been silenced for good, never to be seen again. Kind of sad isn't it?

Monkey Business

I can remember a time when we were given a five dollar bill one time to buy a pair of shoes. This was a luxury to us. We thought we were loaded. So, mom took us to Crown Shoes. In the back of their store they kept a monkey in a very large cage. Meanest monkey in the world!

Anyway, he caught our curious little minds attention, naturally. You didn't think we'd pass this up, did you? At this time we didn't however know that he was mean and nasty. But we did think he was cute, looks sure can be deceiving.

Russell decided the best way to get the monkeys attention was to wave his five dollar bill at him. That monkey grabbed that five dollar bill and ripped it, chewed it, tossed it in the air, like it was an everyday thing. He was having a ball destroying Russell's heart. The store manager was furious at us for teasing his monkey. But to quiet Russell down and keep the rest of his customers in the store, he replaced the five dollars. Then, he rushed us thru our purchases and out the front door personally. We never had such fast service in all our life. Every time we came back to shop he would follow us around, giving us fast service and detour us from the back of the store. He was such a nervous little man. There was no way we were getting near that money hungry little monkey. I kind of feel sorry for the poor man. He must not have children, and now thanks to us, probably never will.

Playing Indians, looks like Russ has the upper-hand

Now I do

Adventures Away From Home

My mother, being the great wonderful mom she is, was always willing to give us another chance. She would still take us with her to do the shopping, laundry, or other things pertaining to risk on her part. This wasn't easy for her, considering all the fights, and boo boos that were always happening. I'll give you a few instances so you can kind of get the picture of what I'm talking about (Send sympathy cards to…)

This trip was for shopping. Sometimes we went inside with mom, and then there were the times when we were bad, and had to stay in the car for punishment. This was one of the latter times. We seem to of had more of the latter times than the going inside times. I think we were near our teen years before we finally made it inside the stores.

Bill and Russ were fighting over whose fault it was we had to stay in the car. I was fighting with Benny over whose fault it was. And then we would switch partners, and start all over again.

While we were settling our differences, Vincent and Tommy were trying to get into the front seat to play with the gear shift, steering wheel, and radio. Now we bigger people are supposed to be keeping an eye on the little people. But as you can plainly see, we had far more important issues to attend to first.

They were helping each other over the seat. Vincent finally made it, and was helping Tommy, when we heard this loud snapping noise. This was followed by Tommy's screaming. This got our attention, fast. A little late, but none the less we were watching now! A new TV for the doctor, he was getting pretty good at broken bones. Of course we gave him lots of practice.

Now comes the part where we have to place blame on someone, so when mom shows up, we can throw her someone. This will leave the rest of us in the clear. (We hoped) Our loyalty to each other usually left pretty fast when mom showed up; smart move on our part. Then it was everyman for himself. We didn't always throw each other to the wolves to save our hides. Sometimes we never confessed and the guilty person would have to be picked in a random drawing. Like; eany, meany, miny and mowed. Or we would all be mowed, which ever the case may be. Sometimes we covered for us so good we forgot who did do it.

Off for another adventure with mom! This time, it was the cleaners. We waited in the car. (Naturally, we were in the back seat.) Mom felt it was safer there. But then, she hasn't been right yet! You guessed it, fighting again. You would think we didn't like each other the way we fight all the time. We did, honest!

Anyway no one noticed that Vincent had crawled over the seat so he could play with all the fun stuff that was call a "no-no". He sure did like that gear shift. I think we noticed him about the same time he was pulling the gear shift out of park and into neutral. Of course he had no idea what he had just done to his innocent family, not to mention all the pedestrians on the sidewalk in front of the car.

The car started to move slowly toward a very large picture window. Boy was it big! Bill grabbed Vincent and pulled him into the back seat. I was jumping over the seat as fast as my little body could go, and shoved my foot down on the brake, pushing down as hard as I could. But it was too late!

By the time that thing stopped we were in the cleaners. "Hi, Mom! We thought we'd stop by and pick you up so you wouldn't have so far to walk. Not buying that huh?! Why is your face so red mom? Honest mom, it was a boo-boo. Alright, I confess, he did it!!!"

Our greatest boo-boo of all time, this even topped the time Tom went out the window of the car in a busy intersection. That was a real biggy until now. I think of these times and wonder how we made it through childhood. Hard heads and a lot of luck I guess. (Mom has her own thoughts on this subject, but she's not at liberty to say. Just in case she needs an alibi someday.)

To elaborate on Tom and the window, it was like this. Tommy was leaning out the rear window of the car, he likes close up views. One of us darling little angels gave a slight push. This was in a busy intersection like I said earlier. Cars were stopping all around us. Mom couldn't understand what the delay was. She's looking all around the area then looks at us; we're looking out the window. She then noticed she was short one child. Upon discovering this happy note, she bolted from the car in search of number four son. She picked him up, looked to see if he was alright, shot us one of those who done it looks, and we started plotting our alibis. We started throwing each other at her mercy. It's a dog eat dog world out there.

Tommy, fortunately for us, as well as himself survived. A few bumps, a scratch or two, but nothing serious. At least not as serious as what we got. We didn't fair so good. Sitting was a problem and a luxury for a day or so. I still can't remember what angel pushed him out the window. There was so much confusion and pushing blame, we forgot. And nobody is talking.

You'd think our behinds would be calloused by now. Maybe they were I know it wasn't getting to Russell like it was the rest of us. We called him iron pants. My dad just said, "No brains, no pain."

Doctors - How We Kept Them Fed

In our younger years we helped keep the doctors well fed, driving the best of cars and vacations in Palm Springs. Nothing was too good for our Doctor's; they earned every penny of it. Besides all that has happened up till this point (omitting the gruesome parts) there were many, many more incidents. I'd need a whole book on accidents concerning unstable children to cover them all. So it's best we only discuss a few of the more common causes for parents to run away from home.

We were quarantined once, when all of us kids came down with Scarlet fever, at the same time. Mom stuck everyone in one room, mine. It was the warmest, the chimney ran through it. In these days doctors made house calls, and he stopped by every day to see how mother was doing. (Kidding mom)

Then we all had measles together, we had chicken pox together, flu, and so on. We always stuck together. We were raised to share everything we got. Fortunately we didn't share broken parts. That's when we drew the line; you were completely on your own with that one.

Being put in close contact with each other had severe repercussions. Try picturing five sick children in one full size bed. Bad stuff is going to happen, especially when it happened to be us. Mom tucks us all in after we have our medicine and tells us to get some sleep. Then she leaves the room and we hear her going down the stairs. It usually only takes maybe two or three minutes before someone breaks the silence and we start down a path we don't want to be on. "Stop pushing me" "I didn't push you, move over" "you move over" "you better be quiet or Mom is going to get you" "you be quiet" "No, you be quiet" "stop shoving" "who took my covers" And somewhere in the bowels of the house we hear those words we didn't want to hear, "Stop talking and go to sleep" "uh oh, now you guys did it" "I didn't do anything I'm sleeping" "no you're not" "I am too" "liar, liar" "You're going to get us in trouble if you don't be quiet" Then we hear Arghhh!! Coming from the bowels of the house where Mom had gone. This is followed by loud footsteps on the stairs and the door being flung open. We look and Mom is standing there with her hands on her hips, and that look in her eyes. We did it now, five kids dove under the covers to hide. You can't hide from Mom's. They know how to find you; they have built in radar to track you down. Mom starts to speak to us in a very low slow tone, this is not good. "It- better- stay- quiet- in – here; – get - to – sleep- *NOW.*" Five tiny voices tell her they will. "Don't make me come back." Very quietly we say, ok. The door closes and we hear loud stomping on the stairs as she disappears into the bowels of the house. We can hear her and Dad talking, "Did you beat them?" "Not yet" "Do you want me to beat them?" "Maybe if they don't settle down and go to sleep soon" "Ok, just let me know if I need to get the belt." Oh no, not the belt, "I don't know about you guys but I'm going to sleep so don't bother me. " Parents have very persuasive ways to get your attention.

Crow attack

When Tommy was one year old, he was attacked by a crow. (The doctor needed a vacation, I think from us.) We were outside playing, when for no apparent reason whatsoever, this huge crow starts to dive bomb us. Maybe the neighbors sent him. It kept coming at us, until it decided that Tommy's head would do nicely.

After landing on his shoulders it started pecking his head. He screamed we screamed, and mom came running, she screamed. We chased the crow away, but by the time Mom got it off of Tommy's head he was bleeding from several pecks. Mom hurried us into the house, put a towel on his head, and called for reinforcements.

When they arrived, mom showed them Tommy's head, and explained what had taken place. They said they needed to catch the bird to see if it was rabid. He wasn't hard to find, he was sitting on top the garage daring someone to do something about it.

Half an hour later they were still at it. Our neighbor stepped out on his porch carrying his over and under double barrel. They laughed at him, and upon sizing him up asked the question of the day. "I suppose you can do better?" In answer, he raised his gun with one hand, and shooting from the hip he dropped the bird right into their laps. You didn't know we had Wyatt Earp living next door, did you? Gasps were everywhere. Tommy took twenty stitches, and a lot of painful shots. Thanks neighbor.

After the crow attack, we got back to normal. Well, as normal as can be expected from us. (What do you want, blood?)

Ben and Vince turned over the motor cycle, and Ben was stuck under it. We tried to get the bike off him before mom found out. But, the yelling caught her attention. That thing must have weighed a ton. Mom and her friend got it off. All he suffered was a bruised leg (warm bottom) he was fine. The bike on the other hand needed to be hid before dad saw it. Unfortunately, we weren't the Hulk.

Ben next stepped on a rusty nail and had to have shots. New doctor, new vacation plans. We fell out of trees, snuck into the fudge, and at all times tried to appear like little angels.

Tommy was bitten by a dog, and then Benny was bitten by a dog, habit forming. Ben was trying to get out of a dog pen after playing with some German shepherd pups. The mama dog didn't take kindly to visitors, and while Ben was trying to scale the ten foot fence, she came after him. She jumped up and bit him on the, OHUMM!! Let's just say he didn't sit comfortable for quite awhile.

Spooky stuff

Remember those wonderful old scary movies? TV shows such as: Shock Theater, Twilight Zone, Outer Limits, and Count Dracula movies. Boy did we like to get scared. What made it even more remarkable was that the TV screen was only 12" across, and yet, in black and white it had the ability to scare little kids.

We would turn out all the lights downstairs. Put our snacks next to our chairs, and get set for the movie to start. We had to be sure that we didn't have to leave the safety of our chairs for the entire length of the movies. If you moved, it was at your own risk.

There is a wise guy in every crowd. Russell was ours. The movie would be half way through, when Russell would very quietly creep across the room looking for his prey. Once he spotted one, he would sneak up behind them so quietly they wouldn't hear him 'til it was too late! He'd reach up and touch your shoulder, then walk his fingers up to your neck, make some groaning noises, and watch you scream and jump up out of your chair. Mixed with the other noises of Papa yelling for quiet, and throwing in a few bodily threats, seemed to quiet us down pretty fast. (Bodily threats?)

As I was saying about the movies, we would pull our chairs up near the television set, and get ready to be scared. We actually had bulging eyes, and goose bumps, and the shakes before the set was warm. This way if the movie wasn't scary enough we would be ready for anything to make us jump. Didn't matter what is was, we jumped. Hello---we were jumping. We also did a lot of scrunching up in our chairs. In this way the monsters had a hard time getting to your neck. Ever notice how they always go for the neck? What's so interesting about a neck? After the first Russell attack, we were prepared for anything. You know how persistent that Count is!

Benny was the most affected by these movies, him being one of the youngest and all. He was a little more impressionable. Little kids believe anything. We would fill his poor little mind full of so much hogwash that it took Mom days, and sometimes weeks to set his mind at ease.

We watched a story on Twilight Zone (I think) one time where a kid disappears threw the wall. This jolted us just a little bit, by the time our imaginations were through with us we were avoiding walls. We didn't want to take the chance of being sucked into the Twilight Zone! So we were a little impressionable too!!! So what, what do kids know anyway? Vampire movies – Impressionable children

Let's talk about Vampires. Kids were crazy about Count Dracula. Well, at least we were. I myself was very impressed. I saw every movie with them I could. I used to watch them so much that I ended up sleeping with my back against the wall and the blankets tightly wrapped around me to keep him from my neck. I even put some tape on the window in the shape of the cross. You know how they are afraid of those crosses. I never could find any silver bullets. OOPPSS!! That's the other guy.

My Dad, knowing I was a vampire freak took us to a triple movie feature at the drive-in. Imagine three Vampire movies back to back - WOW!! My eyes were glued to the screen. Of course in those days you have to remember that the Vampire never survived to make a part two. Our Vampires went out with spectacular dying scenes. The New Vampires live on forever as heroes, go figure.

After watching all three movies I was pumped up and on the lookout for Vampires around every corner. On the way home I kept my eyes on the windows looking for bats, you don't want them creeping up on you. I went to bed without turning on the light. I just changed real quick and jumped into bed. I snuggled under the covers, pulling them up around my neck for protection. I was not prepared for what happened next. I stretched out to get comfortable and my feet felt something moving. It was wet and sticky too. My first thoughts were on -you know who. My imagination went wild. HE'S HERE!!! He's here, and he's going to get me. This is when I noticed that little things were crawling up the sides of the bed and all over the end of it. Something heavy was lying on the foot of the bed and big red eyes were staring at me, making low moaning noises. That's when I started screaming. I wasn't going to let him take me. It was time to call out the cavalry to save me. Mom was the first on the scene with the others tripping over themselves, trying to get into the room to see what had happened.

Someone turned on the light, (good move, wish I'd thought of it) the big bad monster turned out to be my cat. She was laying on the end of the bed calling to her brand new baby's to come to her. When I got into bed some of them fell off, and that is what was crawling up the sides of the blanket. I felt so dumb. Everyone else thought it was hilarious, and told anyone who would listen to them about the monster with the big red eyes. I admit it was pretty silly, but you know at the time something like that is happening, you get pretty wild with the imagination, and can scare yourself pretty good.

Spooks and Halloween

Speaking of spooks and things, it brings me to the subject of Halloween. Boy did we have fun! I mean we really had fun. It wasn't like it is today. There's no fun in it today. Six o'clock comes along and they turn off house lights. Back then we stayed out until they dragged us home. And neighbors all got into the act. They had as much fun as the kids did.

We had the old home made costumes; we could create the most unusual designs. We used pillow cases instead of bags for our loot. (Pillow cases didn't tear if it rained) We covered every house in our neighborhood. Twice!

My brothers made the prettiest women. They had stringy hair, large boobs, stripe socks, short skirts, makeup; the works. By the time the finishing touches were put on they were absolutely breathtaking. I mean, really took your breath away. Except Billy, he would only dress as a cowboy, motorcyclist, or pirate, none of that sissy stuff for him. He wasn't about to ruin his image.

There was one Halloween that I doubt that I'll ever forget. Some friends of ours down the street were having a party. It was given by their oldest son, and they went all out to have real looking costumes. You know the kind - RENTED!

My girlfriend and I were on our way down the road to start our collections, goofing around and having fun. We thought at first that it was a couple of winos, but on further inspection it wasn't. They were loping from side to side, one was swinging his arms, and one was stiff legged and armed. I looked over at her, she looked at me. I said, "We might try cutting threw the field next to us." She agreed. We walked a little further and heard a few growls and groans. This almost convinced us to run. We were hanging onto each other for dear life, moving very slowly trying to get around them. They started to come toward us. Moaning and groaning, then they stepped into the path of the streetlight, and we got our first good look at them. Then we screamed and ran across the field. It was Frankie baby and the Hunchback. We didn't stop to look back till we were on the first road past the field. Then we saw them knock on Bobby's door (the kid with the revenge of the football game plot) he let them in. They looked over at us and waved. We weren't sure whether to laugh or cry the relief was overwhelming.

Or the time I had to babysit on Halloween, and the people went to the party next door. That's when strange monsters kept showing up at the wrong house, and once I was able to get my heart restarted again I was able to point them next door. I saw the most amazing costumes (I hope they were). At first it was unnerving talking to Vampires, Monsters, Mummy's, Frankenstein's, (I think you get the picture) but, after the shock wore off I was able to direct traffic without a hitch.

Scary Tales

Talking about scary stuff reminds me of the times we went to Indiana to visit my dad's sister. We had discovered in our quiet little way, a graveyard out behind their house. My cousins, sensing our courageousness about spooks, told us plenty of ghastly tales. One tale was about a woman who floats around the graveyard at night looking for innocent victims. (Sure!) We weren't falling for that old line. I mean, we weren't born yesterday. So, maybe we were a little radical and full of trouble, but most definitely not stupid.

The other tall tale was about a statue. This statue was pretty large. It was located in the middle of the graveyard, and was heavily damaged by the weather. The tale was that if you were brave enough to kiss her toes you would turn color within twenty four hours. Please give us a little credit!! Truly who could possible believe this? Turn a different color? Certainly not us, we aren't that gullible.

And of course we weren't going to buy any of this nonsense. I guess this is when they decided to dare us. And you know of course that anyone named Sawyer doesn't turn down a dare. (Unless otherwise persuaded) So we took a vote, and it was decided Billy would go first; after all he was our leader.

Billy stepped toward it, and we jumped behind a very large tombstone. We didn't want anything bouncing off him onto us. So we watched him walk up to the statue and look her over, then he looked over at us and winked before he bent down and kissed her toes. You could hear the air being sucked in around us. We were holding our breath waiting for him to turn a color. We waited, and waited, but nothing happened. Not a thing. I knew it, just a stupid joke on us. Never believed a thing they told us after this. And believe me they could tell some whoppers. I guess it runs in the family.

Not done yet! On another occasion everyone got into the act for Halloween. Mom and dad had a most unusual car; it fit right into the spirit of things. It was yellow and black with a red hood (the hood blew off while passing a semi) a gray fender, and a blue door. With all of this going for it, Bill figured, why not!

He dressed it up real cute by putting straw in the hood, and painting eyes on the headlights and bumper, then placing a very large homemade bra on the front grill it looked absolutely adorable. Finding this hard to imagine? Try looking at it longer than ten minutes and we'll nominate your name for the Guineas book on longest time spent staring at ugly. It was pretty spectacular, one of a kind, and all ours.

Russ, Billy holding me; one of their helping hands moments.
I was too little to make any decisions.

All Fun and Games, Until It's Broken

Do you remember all those fun games we played from the time the rooster crowed till we were roped and tied and put to bed? You couldn't keep us inside summer or winter. Once the chores were done we were heading outside to play; kick the can, Simon says, mother may I, hopscotch, jump rope, baseball, football and jacks just to name a few.

Summertime was when we used to have enough hot days together to earn the name with warm beaches, picnics, sunburns, poison ivy and minnows.

Winter on the other hand, had a few advantages also. We would find a place to ride our sleds and toboggans, have snowball fights and ice skating at the pond. You can't do this in the summer. We had a special hill that we used for sledding, and it took all of us to haul the toboggan up it. The ride down was pretty scary, but it never stopped us from going again. The hill was riddled with tree stumps. So on the way down we would hit a stump and kids would fly off; another stump, more kids flew. The goal was to make it to the bottom without falling off. Only the strong survived. Then we would haul it back up, and do it again, until we just couldn't climb anymore.

Of course when we had our dog Flip, we hooked our sled to him instead. He pulled us anywhere we wanted to go, and a few places we didn't- like; bushes, ditches and rocks.

Indoor Sports

We also had our share of indoor sports too. In the colder months Mom hung clothesline in my room. The clothesline was mainly to dry clothes, but my brothers have such clever minds. And before long they had discovered, that if you unhook one end you could then hang on to it and swing to the other side of the room. Just like Tarzan! Being the Tarzan fans they were they had begun to swing from the vines (ropes). This was fine for awhile, but they had a slight problem that brought their swinging days to a halt.

As I picture it again in my mind, Bill was swinging across the room on his vine, and it was just beautiful. He was doing the Tarzan call, and Cheetah was making noise across the room (Russell) and it was just as wonderful. But for some unknown reason to us, Cheetah ran across the room and opened the closet door just at the same time that Tarzan was swinging by, and caught his chin on the top of the door. There he was, hanging by his chin on the door. He hung there for awhile. We were in awe. Our mouths down to our chins, eyes popping open. He just hung there. Shock I guess. He finally moved, jumped down, and as nonchalantly as he could, asked the fifty dollar question, "What Happened?" He then proceeded to touch his chin, found blood, and lost all traces of cool.

Mom had to take him to be sewn up. The swinging days were over, and it was time to move on to other things to do. Unfortunately for Mom, for we had many.

Vincent's washing machine episode. There are some things in life you just have to face all by yourself. Vincent had been fooling around with the wringer washer. He said he was trying to help mom. A likely story, since when did we help? So, he was putting things in the wash, and putting things in the wringer, like his arm. He got a little too close- it grabbed him, and started to stuff him in the rollers.

After a couple of good screams, it aroused our curiosity. When we finally checked it out seconds later, we found Vince trying to squeeze through the wringer.

Well, mom let go with a karate chop to its main point, and it popped open with a loud plop, and threw out his arm. Fortunately, he didn't break any thing; the wringer was going to be just fine. It never worked better. Vincent didn't hurt anything serious. His skin just globed up in about four places and scarred that way, that's all. Terrified him of washing machines, and he wouldn't go near one for a very long time, he was fine.

I think Mom would have preferred book worms at times. (But you know how messy they can be) Nice quiet children, but then she wouldn't have all these wonderful memories, now, would she? Sanity would be nice. And what would she be able to relate to her friends, and analyst?

While the grownups are away!

Mom and Dad were on a bowling league. Every Saturday night they were off to the bowling alley, and we were at it again. (We never really stop, only pause for a moment. NEVER) Five little faces looking out the window watching their parents go off into the night for a few hours of sanity. They thought we were saying bye! Little did they know that within half an hour the house would look like hurricane Mable had passed by, twice!

After we were sure they were gone, and wouldn't return for something forgotten, we'd start operation destruct! Brother Billy was our sitter, he usually gave us the all clear sign.

Being our sitter he taught us all kinds of really neat games. He was our HERO. He made up games such as, Alligator Pond, Quicksand, war, etc. You get the idea.

To play, we had to put all the furniture against the walls. Move the lamps to a place of safety. Then when everyone was all standing in position on the furniture, we would start.

You have to run around the room on the furniture real fast, and if you fell off or lost your footing and fell in; you were out of the game. Anyone eaten by the alligator couldn't play. And if you were drowned it was hard to get out of the Quicksand, so you had to stay put till a new game. So you can see how important it was not to fall in. But, sometimes the guy behind you would accidentally on purpose push you off, so you had to be very careful. This was really lots of fun.

We went all out to make it look real. Russ and Bill got the ketchup into the act a few times. We couldn't use it too often, because it was a little hard to explain why everyone got so clumsy all the time. This was especially tricky if ketchup wasn't on the menu.

To play the war games you start out by putting the furniture in stacks so that the different squads could have a headquarters. Let the War begin.

We had many different kinds of wars. The usual kinds: Cowboys and Indians, just plain War, or Hillbilly's and Hillbilly's. That was a good one. All you needed was a good feud. We'd start them sometimes with corny sayings that all the kids used in school. (Mostly on us) Something like, "You called her a what?" "You heard me stupid; when she sits on a mule you can't tell which one is the mule" "Is that right? Your mother wears combat boots". "Your mother dresses you funny" "Did you buy that ugly suit or did you come by it naturally?" "You must have tripped on an ugly stick yourself." "Beauty is in the eye of the beholder; so what's your excuse?" "Your mother made a rag doll, and now everyone thinks your twins." And off to war we would go. Kids will buy anything.

I think now would be a good time to describe for you Russell's dying act. It is marvelously done, Oscar material. Clasping hands on chest, straighten body stiff, twirl around a few times, for effect of course, fall down very slowly, bring both legs and head up at the same time, kick legs and arms wildly, and then he'd get up and say "You missed me, nah nah! He used to drive us crazy. We'd plan all kinds of ways to get him to stay down once he was. We sat on him a few times, but he'd push us off. Once in awhile he'd stay down just to throw us off the scent. He was lots of fun, all of them were.

Sometimes the enemy would fight about whether you missed them or not. Remember Russell's Oscar nomination? Of course they always missed me. When, you plan out a very complicated strategy and sneak around the yard on your tummy till you can see the whites of their eyes. Then, you rise up and run toward them shooting all the way. (We saw this on TV) They actually have the nerve to stand up very smugly and stare you right in the eye and say. "You missed me, I moved at the last minute, and the blast shot passed me and bounced off the garage." Or "It ricocheted off my belt buckle, see the dent?" It kind of gets to you a little as you stroll back to your headquarters for another plan, saying all the time, "I know I did, I know I did, didn't I?" And they have the gall to stand over there and giggle and laugh behind your back. It's just not fair.

Indian wrestling

My brothers really enjoyed Indian wrestling. Our TV Hero's did, Davey Crocket, Jim Bowie and Daniel Boone. What's good enough for them was good enough for my brothers.

Here is what you do. Lying down head to foot, they would lock legs together and try to flip the other one. Bill was the Champ and Russell was the runner up. I never did it again after the first three times. I'm not too fond of flying. Ask anyone, they'll tell you, "She doesn't let her feet off the ground."

When the boys were older, my dad would challenge them, and sometimes they would challenge him, to no avail. He of course won, but they put up quite a struggle. They had a lot at stake when they wrestled with dad. Because you see, whoever won got to be boss of the house. They tried and tried for years. Oh Well!! Maybe someday they'll have their own house to boss.

Wrestling Oops

On one of our escapades with Bill, "our sitter", things got a little out of hand, or I should say leg! We were being Indians and Cowboys. I was captured by the Indians (Russell's team) and put into a corner with pillows and other stuff over me to hide me, I think. (You don't think they were trying to get rid of me, do you?) Anyway, Benny was trying to rescue me. He had to break into the enemy camp, take them by surprise, and get me out. This was a piece of cake, right?

He was wonderful the way he crawled across the floor (ground) and around the furniture (trees and rocks), and then he was spotted. A fight broke out. Billy and Ben wrestled it out after Russ got it with an arrow, and Vincent got it with a tomahawk. He was on his own, and had to fight the chief alone. Soon the battle was over. They wrestled, they hit, they boxed, and they bit and hit, and hit and bit, but to no avail. The chief won the war and Ben won a butte of a broken leg. Oh well, you can't win them all.

Of course parents aren't in the least interested in the outcome of the war, only in the seat of the pants. Chief warm pants soon found this out the hard way, and a few of the not so brave, braves.

And, remember our homemade toys? We didn't have any of this junk stuff they have today. Falls apart after a week's hard playing. We had sensible toys. Like stick guns, (they lasted practically forever, unless the dog found it) homemade slingshots, tin cans, and other very inventive stuff like that. Why we'd walk along, see something lying on the street, and say to ourselves – "Selves, I think we can play a game with this." Imagination goes along way when cured the proper way.

My brothers had another favorite toy. Snakes. I myself never indulged. I do of course remember a time when I was in the front yard minding my own business. And, I might add, having fun doing so. When Russ came running through the yard lickety split, threw something at me and yelled over his shoulder, "Hold this a minute I'll be right back." I did. I'm very helpful you know. I stood there for a minute watching him disappear down the road with Bill chasing him. Then when I was sure all was well, I took a look at what I was supposed to hold for a minute. SNAKE!!!! I needless to say being a fully fledged tomboy stood very still. Never moved a muscle till Russ came running back through five minutes (an eternity) later, thanked me, took his snake, George, and left. UGH!! Being a tomboy isn't what it's cracked up to be. After this they wanted me to go with them when they went looking for gardener snakes and worms. Like I said, UGH!!

Life continues on with so many adventures it is hard to keep track of them all.

I remember a time when our aunt took care of us while the folks went out to Idaho. We snuck into the candy and she looked everywhere for the culprit. He would have to pay for this crime. We don't know how she knew mom's candy was missing, but she knew. (Mom kept it hidden) Anyway, she caught all of us out by the garage and lined us up against the wall. We thought, "This is it! "Firing squad time". Starting from one kid and moving to the next, she had each one of us open our mouths so she could look inside to see if there was a trace of chocolate left in there. She found none. Maybe we didn't take it? I don't know, nobody confessed, she ate our desert, as punishment. This was an act of cruel and unusual punishment. How did she know where mom hid her candy anyway? And maybe she made it up so she could have our desert! Hmm, could be. Down with tyrants!!!

I must confess we had our good spots too! We weren't always brats? We helped out with some of the chores? We watched the smaller ones on occasion? Plus, we babysat with all the friends' kids, so they could chit chat. Keeping the little ones occupied while mom was busy with her work. We did our share of being sweet. It's just that our brattier days were more consistent.

Our home was located on a dead end street, and at the end was a grove of trees. These trees were to the right of where the road stopped, and lined up in two rows with clear ground in the middle. It was very quiet and peaceful there. This we took over as our place.

At this time of our life Tarzan was our hero. (Next to Billy) No one ever missed a show without a good excuse, if you wanted to stay in the club. Billy always got the part of Tarzan. Nobody wanted to beat him up and take the part away. He was our hero, and heroes have to be treated special you know. Besides, he could beat the socks off of us. He was a strong little bugger.

My girlfriend Connie always got to be Jane. Bill was sweet on her. Her sister Blossom and my brother Benny were quite the twosome for awhile there. She was the cutest little thing with black hair and long lashes.

Russell and I had to take turns being cheetah. Ha Ha you laugh, but, we all have to be or do something ridiculous at one time or another. Oh to be a child free of inhibitions that adulthood brings with it. Not everyone can play a monkey it takes talent. There's more to it than swinging from vines and eating bananas. There's character, attitude, noise, it's not easy being us. We were good at what we did, that's why we got the part. I think?

We spent many hours out there pretending to be in deepest, darkest Africa. We had safari hunts, restless natives, and wild beasts attacking, boy you name it, and we had it. And to make himself be the real Tarzan, Billy hooked up ropes in the trees so he could fly from one to another. He made quite a sight. He was pretty good at it too just like the real one. Johnny Weissmuller was our favorite Tarzan. We loved to hear his calls.

During one of our playtimes I was probably, oh, maybe ten feet up, when mom called us for dinner. I didn't hear her. Billy hollers for me to hurry up and get down so we could go eat. (He doesn't like missing meals)

I did hurry. And I lost my footing. Down I went taking a few small branches with me. You haven't lived till you've slid down a ruff, branch filled, and prickly tree. Fortunately, it was a fairly smooth tree. Thank goodness the ground was there to break my fall, I wanted off this crazy ride. I suffered minor scrapes. (I wouldn't recommend it as a sport if you're thinking of trying it.)

The worst part of it was while sitting on the ground recuperating from my slip'n'slide experience, Bill was standing there laughing like a Hyena. He thought it was rather funny. Then he has the nerve to tell me I didn't have to hurry that fast. He said he would have waited had I preferred to climb down instead. FUNNY! I had to walk bowlegged for a few days after this. But, I did learn a very important thing from this. Never wear shorts if you're planning to slip'n'slide on bark.

Brother Bill, such memories. I can still picture him standing around with his motorcycle boots, jacket, and those crazy hats. He loved hats. It didn't matter what kind. Cowboy, old, new, short billed or long, caps, loved them all. They had a way of adding to his image. He seemed to become what he wore.

Daredevils or just plain dumb?

Bill and Russ did all kinds of crazy and stupid things together -mostly on dares. You couldn't dare them not to do something; they'd do it just to prove a point.

Like, let's say, knife throwing. They called it chicken, I called it stupid. But what do I know, I'm only a girl, and chicken at heart. Russell had his feet spread as far as he dared to without being called out, and Billy still caught his big toe. Then, we had to pull them off each other. Or, the time they jumped off the top of the house to see who could jump the farthest. (It was a two story house) Born daredevils or born dumb, we aren't sure which. They'll tell us someday.

Found money.

Russell and I had come into a small fortune, and were on the verge of spending it one day until greed set in. You know how when you only have so much and you don't want to give any of it up. And besides, how far could a quarter go with five kids?

So, we were trying to get to the store secretly. We were ducking behind trees, hiding under bushes, so on. Then, we were spotted. We took off lickity split with the gang right behind us. The faster we ran, the faster they did. They were gaining on us. Russ yelled to cut across a clearing up ahead. So, when we get close to the clearing he tells me not to cross his lane because we'd trip. I didn't, he did. He was looking back, lost direction, and ran right smack dab into me. While I was laying on the ground yelling in agony; Russ was trying to figure out what to do and left for the store. I was on my own, broken toe and all. So I sat there and smiled as they sailed past me, I waved, and under my breath I plotted revenge. Russell's conscience got to him, he came back to help me. He helped me all the way to the store and back. No sense wasting a quarter! And when we got back to the house he fixed my toe for me. Using Popsicle sticks, he put a splint on it, very professional looking too. I was very touched by it all. This was a side of him I didn't know was there. It was very nice to see. (I won't tell the guys Russell. Your secret is safe, unless they read this of course, then you're on your own.)

Keeping up with the boys

Never having any sisters (thank goodness) I was always competing to do better than the boys. Sports were one field I wanted to try. Unfortunately, they had already stated that no way would they play with a sissy girl. It didn't matter that I could climb trees better, bat better, or fight better. (Brag better) There was no way possible to play. But, things have a way of working themselves out, don't they?

They were sitting around the kitchen sulking about how their football game had to be cancelled. Something about one of the guys going with his mom and would be gone all day. I looked at them and smiled real sweet, and they shook their heads no. They looked at me again and said, "Why not?" At this point I must warn you, I have never played before. I didn't know the first thing about it. Still, I was an eager learner.

Now, our street was on occasion covered with tar, and on other occasions it was covered with gravel. Depending on what the city dropped off at the time. At this time unfortunately, it was gravel.

We headed for the huddle, Bill called the plays. (What are plays?) They would block for me. (What's a block?) I was to get the ball and run for it. (Now that sounds easy.) We got into position. Then they start with this hut stuff; hut one, hut two, hut ninety five, hut four, the ball is tossed, to me! I make a great catch. (I catch well too) Down the road I go. I bumped into a couple of guys and fumbled the ball. Everyone's scrambling for it. Ben grabbed it and I tackled him, boy did I. I knocked him down, wrestled with him, kicked, grabbed the ball and ran for a touchdown. Then they tell me you can't do that. They say their playing touch football. (What's that? A new kind of ball they slipped in on me when I wasn't looking?) They should have told me before I broke Benny's arm, gave Russell gravel itch, and sprained our neighbor kids arm. I mean really, if you're going to recruit a rookie, you should teach him or her, the ropes of the game! Am I right!? YOU BET I AM!!!

Because of this one itsy bitsy incidence I wasn't allowed to play for a long time. I wasn't even allowed to watch them play. Very unfair, considering that I went out of my way to sign his cast. And Ben even humbled himself enough to forgive me. At least I think that was what he did. When I look back, I think I was being set up. They were all starting to look and act a little peculiar to me.

Two months later, they came to me to see if I'd fill in for one of the guys again. SHOCK! And like a fool I agreed. Afterwards I found out they had planned it this way. This was their revenge on me. The day had finally come.

They had told Bobby down the street about my fantastic playing. It was my great ability to cripple an entire neighborhood with a single pounce. He of course had the cure. I don't know why they were so sore. I never got to play after that first game. I mean, let bygones be bygones, I always say.

So the game was planned, and we drew up teams. We huddled and got down to business. Bill was the quarter back – what else- he tossed to Bobby; I headed to tackle him. He stood there on the field waiting for me. Everyone else is pretending to scramble around so all of this wasn't going to waste. They didn't want me catching on none too soon.

He never moved, just stood there, I couldn't believe he wasn't trying to make a run for it. I ran into him head on and immediately bounced off him three feet before landing on my hind quarters. Stunned, I looked at all the laughing hyenas around me. That is when it dawned on me that I had been set up. They knew that he was going to knock me for a loop and a half. Some revenge, fellows. I had to sit on pillows for a couple of days. I had to think of something really rotten to get even. You think they know how to get even wait till I get into the act. All I need is a good plan. Someday!

Dead end Street

Living on a dead end street you don't have too many families to choose from, as far as playmates that is. And some, more than other's tend to be grumps. (With a capital G) You know the ones I'm referring to. We all had them at one time or another.

I can't go into detail about some for fear of law suits, (I told you they were grumpy, didn't believe me, did you?) I'll tell about one of our neighbors, how we were naughty children. Awful bad! And I won't mention any names that should be safe enough. It won't you say? Now, you tell me! (I talk to myself sometimes, but don't worry; I haven't had any answers yet. Actually, some of my best conversations have been with me.)

One of our neighbors had a garden. Several did, but he didn't share. The man knew how to grow food like you wouldn't believe. Maybe you would. We know, because we snuck into his garden after hours, and tasted his delightful goodies.

He never gave any of it away, very stingy man. The neighbors on the other side of us gave us stuff all the time. Of course we helped him plant it, and pick it. (I guess that makes a bit of a difference) But even so, the other guy wouldn't let us help plant so we helped him pick. It was the neighborly thing to do.

Bill taught us (who else) how to sneak to the edge of the garden and get down on our bellies. Then we would crawl through the trenches until we were upon our quarry. Some nights we had muskmelon, and some nights, watermelon, and so on. But mostly, we had muskmelons. These were at the far end of the garden. This meant the most risky, because his house was across the street from them. Capture was forbidden at all cost.

The first time out we crawled all the way out there and were about to filch some melons when the lights came on and a voice told us to leave while we could. This gave us a great desire to move fast. We very promptly fled for our lives, and determined to return for those tasty morsels the next night.

This time we waited till midnight. We were sure he'd be asleep by this time, we hoped! We crawled all the way down there and were about to get us some when it dawned on us, Russ and I, that we didn't know the difference between a ripe one, and a non ripe one. Bill quickly told us to push in on the end; if it gave a little it was ready. So we pushed and picked till our bag was plump, then crawled back home, dragging our bags behind.

Our career with the army intelligence came to a halt one day when flood lights were installed. It wasn't such a great job anyway. The pay was bad and hours were ridiculous. There must be something better to do with ones time than crawl through the mud at all hours of the night?

Fun at the Lake

Summers at grandma's cottage were probably our best times. Just about every weekend Mom would take us out there to swim. Sometimes we'd all pile into the back of the truck on the trip to the lake. Billy would talk to passing motorists, and walkers. He liked to flirt with the girls, and drive the men crazy. He was a real picture standing there with the stranger hat on, and talking to people. They would look back at us like we should have been locked up somewhere, and wondering who let us out. The Zoo Keeper, who ELSE!!

We liked having fun. Acting like a complete fool was one of our characteristics. Of course we didn't think we were being foolish, we were just being kids. And everyone knows how kids are -right? Definition of a kid: Center of attention, always fishing for compliments, the first to take credit for a good think, the last for a not so good thing. That was us.

One time we took the car and Bill sat up front with Mom. Now, to get to the lake, you had to go around a few sharp curves, past a golf course, around a couple of other lakes. Mom took one of the turns a wee bit too sharp causing Billy's door to fly open. So, here we are going around a curve and Bills hanging on for dear life. Yelling for Mom to stop! She did, by slamming on the brakes, thus sending the rest of us flying in all directions. He climbed back in, and we proceeded onward. No big deal.

We were on our way home from the lake one time when Billy let out an awful noise. When we looked, he had this ugly looking thing on his toe. There was a lot of pushing and shoving to get away from Billy and his ugly toe. Mom had to stop the car and look at the toe so we would calm down. After Mom saw his toe she got the salt out. We had these little miniature salt shakers for our picnics, and Mom poured one of them right on the big ugly thing. After a few minutes it finally gave up and dropped off his toe. Mom threw him out. The bloodsucker that is, not Billy. Then she proceeded to clean his toe, and bandaged it, then drove us home. By now you see, nothing bothered mom. We had conditioned her to the very real world. So sad.

Mom was pretty used to us having problems, and she took them in stride. It's afterwards in the privacy of your own room that you fall apart and disappear never to be seen again. Then when relief is moments away, a familiar knock appears. Knock, Knock, "Mom, are you in there? Pause…"I can hear you breathing. Come on, we know you're in there." And somewhere deep inside the room you hear this. "There's nobody hear but us chickens." "We don't have any chickens." "I adopted them this afternoon." And you can hear them outside the door talking. "Don't go in there; mom's having one of her moods." And they tip toe away very quietly. PEACE!!!?

My Great Uncle Jim was loads of fun. He had a couple of boats. And he took us out in them all the time. We especially liked his speed boat. He would rev it up so that the front was sticking out of the water. Then he would turn the boat causing it to tilt at such an angle, the water would leak in over the edge. We'd all scream, and he'd laugh, and we all had fun… No matter how much he tried to scare us, we never said no to a ride in his boat.

My mom and Great Uncle Jim tell the story about how he taught her to swim, to just about anyone who will listen. And she is a very good swimmer. He took her out when she was very little, and threw her over the side. He was prepared to jump in and save her if need be, but Mom started kicking her legs and the next thing you knew she was swimming. He taught a lot of the kids to swim. He always said that the younger you start the better. When their older they tend to fear the water. That's my problem. I tend to fear it a lot.

Fear of water

Bill, Russ and I walked over to the beach so they could play on the dock. I waded in the shallow area while they swam. They fortunately knew how. Bill thought he would teach me like uncle Jim taught mom. (Have to watch what you tell to gullible minds like ours) So, he pushed me off the dock, at which point I sank like an anchor. I fought my way to the top only to sink again. When I came up for the third time Billy jumped in and pulled me out. I guess I'm a slow learner. Since then I've been slightly terrified of water. Although I have to admit, I have learned to swim on my back. That in itself is a miracle. (Of course someone had threatened to throw me into a bunch of seaweed if I didn't swim.) I think that is called motivation.

Back at the cottage

Grandpa had put three huge rocks in the lake as markers for the drop off. They were placed ten feet apart from each other when you could see the third rock it was a warning for you to turn back. Only those who were excellent swimmers or half fish could go past the rocks. It was very scary out there the water was so black you couldn't see anything, and it was really cold. Why we would even go near it was way beyond my thinking.

But, we did have a lot of fun with those rocks. No surprise, we invented a game to play with them. Starting with the first one we would play king on the rock. The winner would be able to choose his position on the next rock. We would try really hard to be the winner, because the third rock was very tricky and scary. By the time we reached the third rock we were getting pretty scared. We would hold hands so no one could go over the edge and be lost forever. We would head back to shore after terrorizing each other. To be honest, we would never admit this, we were sorry we invented the stupid game in the first place, but didn't want to be the one to admit it. Fear like that helps you to appreciate the shallow water and playtime with the minnows. It was fun for a while; I think that kids like things better if there's a risk in it. We did. But then we weren't the brightest bulbs in the bunch either.

The grownups were fun to watch as they played in the water. We would take a break and lie on a blanket on the grass and watch them play. Change of roles. Sometimes we joined and sometimes we watched. There just as crazy as we are. I don't know where they got the idea that we were so bad. Look at them for Pete's sake. SHEEESSS!!!!

Our Imaginations on Overdrive

One advantage of having parents interested in bowling is that you get to bowl on occasion. (This was after we were much older and were now able to be safe in public places) We would watch them and learn. Mom and Dad were pretty heavily into bowling, being on the league and all. They won a few trophies, plus, they looked forward to the banquets at the end of the Bowling League.

My brothers and I would cut thru the woods behind our house (before the freeway was put in) to get to the bowling alley. Bill and Russ spent a lot of time there, improving their aim I'm guessing. They were pretty good. Russ had, and still does have, a power line drive when throwing the ball. When it connects with the pins you can hear thunder- loud thunder. This is how he bowls. He swings the ball backwards till it reaches his shoulders, (and that's a long haul if you knew how big he was) then he brings it forward with great speed and sets it free to fly halfway down the alley before it touches the lane, plowing into the pins, and scattering them everywhere - Strike? He has thrown them so hard he has jammed the machine. He even split a pin or two or three. In spite of his handicap, he is an excellent Bowler.

Bill on the other hand, liked to clown around with the ball. He loved trying different ways of getting the ball to the pins. Things like sitting down and rolling the ball backwards, under the leg, blindfolded, etc. You get the picture. The list is endless. You name it, he'd try it. If we mentioned a new way or said, "How about," he'd try it. He was so much fun or was he just nuts, can't remember now.

Bill and Russ had contests to see who could bowl the best. But in these contests you couldn't bowl the regular conventional way, which they seldom did anyway. Needless to say Mom, Dad and the rest of us sat at a table nearby and watched. This way you can cheer them on without using names, and nobody will know the difference. You just yell "Come on long legs you can do it." Things like that. You don't want it getting around that you're with them. People try to avoid you, whisper behind your back, all those childish things. They can't handle all that talent, or don't want to.

Dreams

Does your group sit around talking about their dreams hoping someone will know a guru somewhere with all the answers? Ours did on occasion. I gave up trying to figure people out. Most of their stories were so ridiculous that you either died laughing anyway or were bored silly. And some made absolutely no sense at all. But none the less they would dissect them to see if they should be doing something or receive some great wisdom.

So one thing led to another and I told one of mine. I was dreaming about ships, war, bombs, torpedoes and the other things that accompany that kind of stuff. And for some reason not quite clear our neighborhood was under fire. Don't ask me how a battleship got on land to attack, because my dream left that part out. King Kong probably dropped it off on his way to the coast. I don't know. But there it was, big as life. And it let go of a torpedo aimed right at our kitchen wall. I could see it crossing the street and the yard next door heading for us. It hit the wall and stuck there. Didn't go off, just stuck in the wall.

So I rushed for the kitchen thinking if I get there right away I could disarm it. (Now you got to admit, that is funny, a twelve year old disarming a torpedo.) What a hoot. I'm up out of bed running down the stairs through the house screaming at the top of my lungs, "Man the lifeboats, we're going down," Mom woke me as I entered the kitchen. This was highly embarrassing. You know we never did figure out what it meant but, it made for another great story for the parents to tell their friends. Glad to oblige.

Science

Bill loved to make smelly stink bombs. If your child ever puts on a sweet face and begs for a science kit, don't give in. It's a matter of life and breath, yours. The health risk is far too great. And besides, you would only live to regret it in the long run, should you be so lucky!

Mom and dad gave into his sweet smiling face, his pleading voice, and broke down and bought him one. He told them of the hours of quiet they could enjoy, and how it would keep him busy and out of their hair. He failed to mention that instead of their hair, he'd be infiltrating their sinuses, clothes, and the very air they breathe.

It started out with ROTTEN EGGS!! From then on it was downhill picking up speed all the way. We didn't know that there were so many things in the world that could smelled so bad. He showed us all of them. I should say let us smell all the things we wanted to miss out on in just ten easy experiments. I myself did not find running out of the house gasping for clean air fun. And when for some reason unknown to us, his kit came up missing no one had any idea where it went. Nor did they want to know. No-body formed a search party to retrieve it either. And believe me, when I say it was definitely not in the dissecting room. We had our suspicions, but we'll cover for you Mom. Your secret is safe.

The Artist

Tommy was an artist in his younger years. He took after Mom. Tom painted everything in sight with, anything he could get his hands on. He painted the corner of the house red! Would have painted more, but he was put out of work when Mom spotted him. He did quite a bit of damage before his brush was halted in mid-air. I think he covered a four or five foot area right on the corner of the house (near the front, which stuck out like a sore thumb). Out where all your friends could get a good look. They would ask who the dumb kid was with the Leonardo genes, at which point you played dumb or lied.

On the other hand there is a long line of artists in the family. Not public artists, but the kind that paint in secret at home. Mom is an excellent artist. We kept telling her for years that her talent was being wasted. But then like I was saying before about Mom, she can do anything she sets her mind to. She would be out shopping, see something she liked, and study it a couple minutes, then go home and make it. That's all there was to it. Look, study, do. So it was no wonder that Tommy was following her steps. (well, somewhat he just needed a little guidance.)

He also painted the car with gasoline. Unfortunately, he wasn't spotted as soon this time, and the car ended up peeling. It looked like a bad case of sunburn, and the patient was blistering and peeling all over his body. This was not one of his more memorable experiences. His painting career was nipped in the bud, before it had a chance to flourish, and he went on to become known worldwide, as King of Graffiti. Aren't we the lucky ones?

Back to the olden days as my son calls them. Mom and dad heated our home with a pot belly stove. It promoted togetherness. Nowadays that is not unusual. But when I was little, we were unique. The only people within a hundred miles with a pot belly stove. It was enough to keep a two story house warm, provided you used four quilts and your coat to supplement the heat. We found if you keep in the body heat your fine till morning. The problem we had was leaving enough room for the air to get in. Those little peep holes are a vital thing for your health, not to mention a long life.

Many a time I woke up relieved that I woke up. Gasping for air and sucking in blankets is not the most sought after sport in the world you know. There are other things most of us would prefer doing. Like chopping wood, or hauling wood, or carrying buckets of cinder ash outside to be dumped, at least this way you were secure in the knowledge that heat was soon coming.

My father was a great one for volunteering us for work. He picked his volunteers. We worked pretty hard trying to fill that truck bed with fresh cut wood. My brothers fortunately went most of the time. I only had to go if they were short handed. But all of us helped to unload it and stack it neatly.

We worked hard while at the same time anticipating the hot cocoa and toast waiting for us at home. Mom always had this for us to help warm us up when we returned. That stove was pretty nice to have around unless someone backed into it, or pushed you so they could get closer. We were always pushing someone away so we could get closer. And if you got too close the air changed around you. You could sniff it, and track down the smell only to find it's your pants, not mom's new room deodorant.

Flying Insects

In the summer around our home there were an awful lot of bees and wasps. It didn't matter where you were, you could be guaranteed to be stung. They had contracts out on the Sawyer clan. Russell was stung in his mouth while he was running. The bee flew in and was immediately spit out. What a way to go. The worst part was when Mom tried to make it better by putting her famous cure on it, mud. The moral of this story is – don't run with your mouth open, you never know what your 'e leaving yourself wide open for.

I was stung by accident one time. Something was crawling around my neck, and when it got to my chest I smacked it. It smacked me back. I thought it was a fly! Honest! I tell you they were everywhere. I think they had declared war on us. They fly by in their squadrons on the look-out for prey when they spot us and they say to themselves, "That looks like a healthy group of prospects; let's see how loud they can yell and how fast they can run." They were so thick that we were sitting on them, stepping on them, and standing on them. (Sitting on them wasn't preplanned as a war strategy, it was an oops! I didn't look first kind of thing.)

Grandpa's Shop

My grandfather had his own box shop where he made boxes for greenhouses. We helped him sweep up the sawdust from around the large saws to keep the place tidy. Sometimes, when he had a large order he would let us pull nails from crates or put boxes together. Not too often on the boxes, because he was very fussy about them the nails were supposed to go in straight not sticking out the side. We helped with the clean up, and that was an all day job in itself. There were piles of dust on the floor constantly around the saws.

I was so involved with my sweeping one day that when I stood up I found that; 1: The ceiling was lowered or 2: I'd grown considerable, because my head met an immovable object. A steel bar coming out from the table saw. I can't remember how many times Grandfather had told me to watch out for it. It put a very nice dent in my head. Grandpa was so upset that I was hurt that he cut the bar off the saw right then and there. I wasn't sure if he expected me to repeat it or if he had intended to all along. I was inclined to be accident prone so I would assume this had a lot to do with his actions.

My brothers and I were playing hide and seek at the shop in an area we were told not to play. I split my elbow open while backing into a sheet of glass. Grandpa got rid of the glass after this. I felt like a magnet for spotting hazardous material. This wouldn't have been too bad had it not been for the fact that it was Easter Sunday, and I was wearing a pure white dress. (Used to be white)

Trying to stay out of trouble

I was always getting hurt one way or another. Like when I was riding a bike one day, minding my own business, when this dumb kid grabs hold of the handlebars, and the bike stopped, and the kid I had on the handlebars and myself went for a short flight. Bounced off the gravel and dirt, swooshed threw the puddles, and came to a painful stop, ten feet down the drive. The two of us chased him down and had our revenge.

When I helped dad, I usually stayed out of trouble and pain. Of course all I did was wash car parts in gasoline and hand him tools when he needed them. Taking motors apart and putting them back together. I just helped, like a gofer. But in watching and lending a hand now and then, I picked up a few valuable pointers that help out quite a bit now. My brothers helped much more than I, and have turned out be very good under the hood of a car. Thanks dad

So you remember all the pets you had? We kept our parents busy especially yours truly. I love cats, and was forever finding strays to bring home. I found one on the way home from school one day. I picked it up, fell in love with it immediately, and took it home. Knowing full well Dad would skin me alive for bringing it home. (That was a favorite expression of his) Mom told me that she doubted if Dad would let me keep it because we had so many animals already. My Dad is partial to dogs.

So, anyway, I was prepared for Dad when he came home. I had my coat and boots on, and was patiently waiting for him to walk through the door. Dad came home and Mom filled him in about my determination to keep the cat. So he looked at me holding the cat and he smiled and played with it. I stood there in front of Dad, and I was determined to have my voice heard. I told him, if I couldn't keep Velvet, (I had already named it too) I was going to run away from home. Dad smiled down at me, and gave me a big hug, the cat was mine! Oh, to be little again.

This probably wasn't easy for him to do because we already had a cat and two dogs, one pregnant. But like I said, Dads are human too, they also understand their children. They have to be wise when their children are fighting, part time doctors just like Moms. Also, when your spirit is hurt they have big strong arms to wrap you in, delivering comfort that only Dad's can do. Dads are to be feared and respected. But you should never forget they are human inside, and by the same token never let them forget it either.

My Dad the doctor helped me with a knee injury during my tender years. I don't believe a doctor would have been quite as gentle as he was. I had found a knot on my knee and it kept getting bigger and bigger. It was irritating, so as any child would do, probably,

I picked at it making it very sore. While I was busy picking at it something sharp inside my knee scraped my finger. Oh no, that can't be good.

I showed Dad and he went into action right away. He had Mom bring him some cotton, tweezers and antiseptic. Then very gently he went to work to remove whatever had lodged in my knee. He found a piece of glass in it. He said I must of fell on it some time back, and it was just now working its way out. So he cleaned it up very gently then dressed it, and gave me a hug. He was so gentle and loving. Thanks Dad.

I bet your wondering what my dad looks like huh? Well I'll tell you anyway. He is six feet and some, weighs little more than a tree branch. He is a Charles Bronson look alike, almost. Very likeable, and at times he is very warm, and then there are times he is like a grizzly bear. (I bet your remembering the Bermuda shorts forget It; all exaggeration, dad might be looking over my shoulder)

Another part of a father's duty is to conduct search party's for their wandering children. We wandered most of the time. Well, stuff would catch our eye and we just couldn't help ourselves, off we would go to investigate it. This usually happened in the grocery store or in large department stores, but could occur most anywhere. We had a knack for picking just the right place, for operation disappear.

Brother Ben disappeared when Mom went to pick Dad up from work. My father worked at a salvage yard. When they returned to the car to leave, Ben was gone. "Where did he go?" Who?" "Ben." "Oh him! I don't know, he was here a minute ago, did you see him Vince?" "Not me, how bout you Billy?", "Nope, not me, haven't seen him since we parked, just been sitting here mind-in' my own business" Dad, "Knock it off you screwballs, they're a bunch of screwballs, you know that don't you? We're raising a bunch of screwballs." Father already having put the guard dogs out, was not pleased to have to put them back in their cages. Especially when they thought people were an appetizer. It took an hour to find Ben sleeping in a car in the back of the yard. His dreams were interrupted momentarily when Dad warmed his seat.

Somehow we grew up

We grew up finally. And there were times when we thought that was going to take a miracle. But we made it! I didn't know for sure what was going to be better, but we looked forward to it anyway. I think my brothers had more fun though. They had to accompany me on my dates as my chaperon. My dates liked them better. I not only had a boyfriend, but two lucky brothers. And when I dated, I was escorted to such lavish places as the lake for fishing or the bowling alley, and better yet the movies with the boys hanging over the seat drooling popcorn, and coke hollering such obscenity's as would cause a sailor to faint dead away. "You know these boys?" "What boys? Oh those boys never saw them before in my life." "Then you won't mind if we get rid of them?" "Okay, I admit it, there mine, their out on a pass, I have to get them back soon anyway."

It's not that I didn't like these places or that I didn't like my brothers. I adored my brothers, and bowling and fishing. It's just not the kind of date you grow up hearing about. They weren't romantic, but then my dad didn't want that. How cleaver he must have been. And besides, Billy and Russ were a lot of fun. Ask my dates! They are the biggest cutups (besides me of course) that I knew of. And we kind of liked having them around. At least if you had a flat with them around they were witnesses. The folks had to believe you then.

The grownups got a bigger kick out of us as we grew, and grew, and grew. And when we had finally reached puberty or whatever it is they pat you on the back for, they greeted us with open arms.

In these open arms you would most likely find a number of interesting things. Such as an axe for cutting fire wood, or a dish towel, a mop and bucket, a frying pan, broom, and of course a choice. You can either clean your room today or tomorrow we will have open house for the entire neighborhood. Let them see how messy you are. This usually works even for the hard to convince. The chores I preferred were things like, feeding the dogs and cats, or running to the store for something, these were much easier to relate to. Nothing physical just keep it plain and simple. Our energy was for far more important things, such as dancing, and walking to the malt shop. That takes a lot of strength. And if you use up all your energy on work, you're a dull boy or girl. And if you don't use your energy on work, you're a sore boy or girl! Some choices!

The Big Move

In my teen years we moved to Fenton where we lived for the better part of a year. They couldn't handle us back there anymore. This was like being moved to the boonies for us. Fenton is a very small town. And we didn't feel the people were friendly to outsiders, so things were a bit tough at first trying to fit in. But then again most of our life had been tough, so this wasn't news. We made the best of a bad situation. After all by now our skin was getting pretty tough. So we set out to make new friends, and get ourselves settled in. After some time we were able to establish relationships with other kids in the neighborhood, helping us to feel better about the move. It was hard on us to leave the only home we really ever knew.

We had a few problems with our house being haunted though. I can hear you now. Oh! Really! Yep, sure did! This was a little unnerving. I know what you're thinking. Your thinking that most people who move to a new location think their house is special, and so must be haunted. Right? Wrong. This house most surely was.

My room seemed to be the target and nobody else wanted it. They figured that it was bad enough that I had to sleep with the ghosts, with my head buried under the blankets, that it was too much to expect them to do the same. So they teased me and stayed far away from my room. You can see that they had my back.

Billy used to tease me the most about it. Said my imagination had run amuck with me. He said nothing was there and he would prove it. So one day after we'd been in the house for awhile he was ready to bet on it. That night I slept on the sofa, and he had my room. For approximately one hour and fifteen minutes. This is when I heard him running down the stairs yelling that he isn't going back in there and to give him back his bed. Expressing that there was no way possible to get him back in that room, and he never did.

Later on when he was able to compose his usual cool self, and stop his shaking long enough to relate his story, we were able to find out what happened.

While laying there trying to go to sleep, he had looked up at the foot of the bed and saw two people standing there looking at him and talking to each other. He couldn't hear them but could see they were talking. Then they started to move around the room but they always came back to the middle of the room and stood watching, about this time his hair was ready to stand straight up, and he felt like he was turning white. And he jumped up and out of the room. He didn't see anything I hadn't seen before. But he was scared. (So was I) But they didn't visit every night so it wasn't too bad. They weren't imposing on my hospitality. Very polite of them don't you think?

About a month after Bills leaping the stairs feat, I had my first premonition. I can't say for sure that's what it was, but it happened just the way I saw it. So I guess it was. I told you it was a fun house.

I hadn't been able to sleep, and found myself in the kitchen at two in the morning fixing coffee. And as I was sitting there minding my own business, and trying to solve the problem that was bothering me at the time, which was insomnia from working two shifts, when the ceiling decided to bounce around. That's right- bounce. Bet you haven't seen too many bouncing ceilings in your lifetime? Me either! I guess you shouldn't look at ceilings when you're half asleep and suffering from insomnia. But there it was, bouncing around. Actually it was like the ceiling was breathing. But then a breathing ceiling is worse than a bouncing ceiling both being ridiculous. And we all know that ceilings don't breath anymore than they bounce, do they?! This couldn't be happening. I'll wake up in a minute and it will all seem so silly.

It shook me up enough to have me gulp down hot coffee and make a run for it. I thought the whole cotton picking thing was going to land on me. And I of course didn't want to be around when it decided to let go.

Next morning Mom and I were talking at the dining table and the subject came up rather subtlety. I told her that I expected to walk down the stairs and see the ceiling on the table. And, when she asked the obvious question, why? I took the opportunity to jump into my story. I figured it was good for a few laughs. She thought it was fascinating to say the least. I had her curiosity on high alert. Mom went thru the rest of the day keeping an eye on the ceiling. (Me too)

Around supper time I started to have the awful feeling that something just wasn't right and hurried up with dinner. Vince was the only one left at the table. Everyone else had other plans and so they gulped and left. (Cowards!) So there we were, Vince and I. I was, enjoying my coffee and he was finishing dinner. When he stood up to leave the ceiling fell on his end of the table covering his plate and chair, and the table. Some landed on him but he wasn't hurt. Mom and I exchanged quick glances with each other. There must be something to this premonition stuff. This wasn't to be my last encounter with it.

The Parking Meter Project

My brothers never quit. It was always one thing after another, could not keep up with them. Always in some kind of trouble, big, little it didn't matter. It sought them out and dragged them to where it was. And of course their innocence was not to be taken lightly, so sincere, and remorse. Desperation at its peak.

Their parking meter episode would be a good place to start. As I remember, the story goes something like this. They were walking along shoving each other, whistling at the girls, when they just happened to bump into a parking meter. On bumping into said parking meter they immediately noticed that it moved. Now we all know that parking meters don't move. They just stand around all day swallowing pennies – nickels and dimes. But, trust me on this one they don't move.

It suddenly dawned on them that if moved enough it might fall over. So of course they needed to try out their new theory. And upon this thought they nudged it just a bit with an unobserved kick. It took oh -maybe, five or six good kicks to accomplish this before it fell over. And oh my! They say to themselves we can't leave litter lying around the sidewalk. We must get rid of this garbage. Now where can we take it? I know! We'll take it home. And they did. Sweet little darlings are now going to involve their loving family in it.

Of course we have no need for a parking meter in the living room. Can you see it, five cents to sit for an hour? Standing room is a dime, and penny a minute for talking. It could be hazardous to your health. (Not to mention your wallet)

So they decided to take it to their new dissecting room, the basement. They turned that meter into a pile of steel so fast it made your eyes hurt just to watch. They disposed of it in dad's trunk, for him to get rid of or get caught with it. And now we're all accessories after the fact. Thanks much!

On returning to town to spend their new found wealth, they found the streets busy. The high school was having their homecoming parade. The streets were filled with Fenton and Holly kids.

The missing meter had been noticed – I don't know why? So now the police were busy questioning kids. Bill and Russ wandered over by a couple of police and let it slip that they saw a couple of Holly kids running with the meter. So they gave a few phony I.D.s of them and went on their way.

After a couple of weeks of searching Holly kids they paid a visit on Bill and Russ. And of course they insisted they pay for the meter, and replace the money. (I always wondered how they knew how much money was in it.) It turns out one of their friends had squealed on them. I guess crime doesn't pay. The cost of all this was $86.00. Face it boys, Bogie you're not!

Try as they might some kids are hard to teach. The boys took a gunny sack into a cornfield to get some corn for Mom. (They thought Mom would appreciate this gesture of love.)

Low and behold, before them stood a very large Brahma Bull. Talk about shock treatment. This was the ultimate moment. They inched backwards for a moment or two trying to decide whether or not to panic. I don't think the bull would have cared one way or the other, because he was already snorting and stomping. He didn't need an invitation to join the fun. In fact, he had already decided what he was going to do, and I guarantee it wasn't for their benefit.

They both grabbed the bag of corn and beat a path for the nearest (barbed wire) fence. Stopping at the fence they both pushed and shoved the bag of corn over the top. Now is where the problem comes in, how to get two kids over a fence before the bull helps them spread their wings.

They inched up the bottom of the fence and while one held it up the other one crawled under and then the one safe, held it while the other one crawled to safety. Grabbing their bag they made a beeline for home, all ripped to pieces, covered with multiple lacerations, and their corn. (Which incidentally not knowing the whole story, Mom ended up canning.)

Life goes on sometimes! Mom caught Tommy smoking out behind the garage one day. We heard her yelling and carrying on, so we took a peek to see what the problem was. We thought she fell into a hole or something, but there she was pulling Tommy toward the house by the ear. OWWWW!! He looked like he was going to be sick. By the time they reached the dining room, Tom was searching for a place to hide. There was no way he could have gotten away from Mom even if he had an army to back him up.

You see Mom figured if she couldn't keep the first three from smoking, she was going to give it one last shot with Tommy. She intended to win this time around.

Mom plopped him into a chair and stuck a cigarette into his mouth and told him to eat it. Our mouths dropped open. Had we heard right? Our sweet, gentle mother saying words like that. We were in shock! Had we pushed her too far this time?

Reluctantly, and with a great deal of effort, he ate it. We couldn't watch. He turned all shades of green and blue and looked like he was on the verge of losing his stomach. He swallowed. After a few minutes of silence his color started to return to normal. Everyone was waiting to see how he was. He looked up at mom, and very politely asked for another. Our mouths dropped open again, the hinges weren't working right. Mom threw up her hands and sent him to his room. He actually liked them. Sometimes psychology doesn't work. Or maybe Tommy was using reverse psychology on Mom. He was pretty smart so we wouldn't put it past him to come up with something as clever as that. The thing is we aren't sure if it was because of mom's genius or if he really couldn't stand doing it. Either way I'm glad he stopped smoking.

Stress Tests for Couples

I was thinking that it might be a good idea if couples had to take a stress endurance test along with the blood test before marriage. This would determine if you could leap over a running child heading straight for you at top speed, dodging toys, bikes, clothes, mislaid pets. There should be a time test to see how long it takes you to wash walls, doorways, windows, and ceilings when you're expecting your mom to drop by. (Faster for mothers in law)

Then you have your high pitched screeching noise test. This will determine if you go at an early age or if you will last till it won't be noticed anyway. (Then you sign a contract stating that your spouse can't put you away for at least two weeks. Long enough to find a housekeeper)

If you pass all the above requirements you will be awarded the highest medal of achievement that a housewife has ever earned. And will be given instructions on how to barricade your home, because your services will be sought after by moms from all across the country.

Grown up and a family of my own

I was told once, that the best way to a happy child is to hide the candy, and push the peanut butter. And of course I fell for it. But then I usually bought anything if it sounded kid proof.

Now this will work fine until they discover that you can also paint the refrigerator, table and chairs, kids, and so forth with it. It opens up a whole new world for them. And unless you like having your home painted in the latest peanut butter designs, you will quickly move on to greater and better ideas to keep the little darlings happy, and out of mischief.

Anything will be better than watching them jump off the top of bunk beds landing on a single pillow or their brother, climbing up door frames, jumping on the furniture, filling up the tub and dropping all of your freshly laundered towels in it, and last but not least, taking your favorite cologne – baby powder and shampoo, mixing them all together on the shelf of your linen closet for you to stumble across. The list is endless! You just have to put your nineteen hours (minimum requirement, depending on how many children you have) a day in, and at the end collapse on the sofa, and listen to the quiet for approximately twenty five seconds, long enough for hubby to notice you're not busy. Then you can start waiting on him.

He very lovingly watches you fall into the chair or on the sofa. His heart goes out to you; he feels compassion for your long and tiring day. He expresses it with, "Hard day honey?!" And you get a small nod and groan out. He smiles sweetly. Then it starts. "Honey while your up could you get me a cup of coffee?" Now you of course feel as though the Pittsburgh Stealers have just stomped over your entire anatomy, twice, and here's this turkey sitting here for the last two or three hours resting and taking it easy asking you to get things for him. He wants to play cards, or some other type of game, he wants this and that, on and on. He's had such a rough day, poor thing, he just needs to rest he is really pooped! EASY GIRL! Remember, nerves of steel, you can handle it. After all you've chased four kids all day, one who refuses to wear clothes and runs around the house. You can handle the biggest kid of all. After all tomorrow will be a brighter day. If tomorrow would only show up early, like today!

Are you feeling secure in the knowledge that you are not alone yet? Hundreds of moms and dads everywhere just shared your day with you. (Now isn't that a sobering thought?) Most important of all, are the memories of my family. Looking back at all the touching times, as well as the rough ones, helped me to become who I am today. Thanks for being my family. You helped me to develop a sense of humor for this crazy fast paced world we live in, and to cope with day to day problems with a level head.

CHILDHOOD ----- DON'T LEAVE HOME WITHOUT IT!!!

Acknowledgments

Russell has a family of his own now. He has five children, one girl! He lost his wife to cancer a few years back. His kids have kids now as well. Vincent was married and had three children, one girl! He is now remarried and she has grown kids. But they count too. Jimmy is now James and has a partner. Ben was in the service so long we weren't sure if he was ever coming home. But he finally did, and married and divorced and remarried. He had five children and broke the curse with two girls, divorced and remarried, and divorced, again, lots of bad luck.

In fond memory, we lost Billy in Vietnam in 1968 on my 18th birthday. He died a hero protecting his platoon. We lost Tommy a year later; he was hit by two cars while waiting to cross the street, taking him from us just before he turned thirteen. We miss them both dearly.

Our greatest loss was when we lost Mom in May of 2006 to cancer and we miss her oh so much. My Dad is still with us and doing well, I cherish every day with him.

Mom, Dad, Billy, Russ and myself with two cousins

Mom and Dad

Grandma and Grandpa

Me and Grandpa

Mom on the bike

About the Author

Thelma A.P. Krzyszton lives with her husband Mark, and dog Molly, in a modest home in Michigan. Coming from a large family and then having one of my own, has helped to form the woman I am today. This is my first book hopefully not my last.